# Remade

## A LIFE OF HOPE AFTER DOMESTIC VIOLENCE

### Shannon Dorsey

Published by
Our Written Lives, LLC

Our Written Lives, LLC provides publishing services for authors
in educational, religious, and human service organizations.
For information or to submit your manuscript, visit
www.OurWrittenLives.com.

Library of Congress Cataloging-in-Publication Data
Shannon Dorsey
Remade: A Life of Hope After Domestic Violence

Library of Congress Control Number: 2019910834
ISBN: 978-1-942923-41-1 (paperback)

Scriptures are from the King James Version of the Bible.

# Remade

## A LIFE OF HOPE AFTER DOMESTIC VIOLENCE

Shannon Dorsey

# Foreword

GENESIS 50:20
. . . Ye thought evil against me;
but God meant it unto good.

Remade is the perfect title of the book to tell the story of an amazing woman that I have the privilege to call my wife. I watched Shannon change from a woman that was scared, confused, depressed, and hurt into a lady that knows who she is, understands her purpose, and is fulfilling God's will for her life.

This book uses pen and paper to paint a portrait of the resilient, evolving life of Shannon Dorsey. Of course, there is more than one side to every story, but this story is told through her eyes.

The Bible tells us that we overcome by the blood of the Lamb and the word of our testimony. Looking back to tell your story brings glory to God. As Joseph looked back on his life, he said in Genesis 50:20, "But as for you, ye thought evil against me; but God meant it unto good."

God has helped Shannon forgive the past and appreciate the place it brought her to, and we believe as she shares her story she will help save someone else.

I applaud Shannon for writing a book that talks about real issues and situations that people go through, yet rarely talk about. Many people try hard to be perfect, or at least to present a perfect image without ever really being able to be themselves or appreciate who they are. Hopefully, this book will help someone understand that no one is perfect regardless of the image presented.

The truth is, just because we aren't perfect doesn't mean we can't be used to impact the world. You may be a broken vessel, but as long as you stay in the Potter's hands, He will make you over and continue to place you in position to increase His Kingdom.

Although Shannon's life was marred and she was broken in many ways, God has used her to be a great mother, teacher, friend, youth leader, pastor's wife, and much more!

We hope this book will bless you in whatever place you are at in your life, and that as Shannon tells her story the Lord will strengthen, and encourage you.

The life you were born into shaped you. What you went through in your past brought you to your present. I believe God is using what you are going through right now to bring you into your destiny.

*Jason Dorsey*

# Contents

# Introduction

ROMANS 8:28
And we know that all things work together
for good to them that love God, to them
who are the called according to His purpose.

My name is Shannon Dorsey. People who know me say the first thing they notice about me is my smile. I haven't always been the person I am today; I've become an individual that actually loves life. It hasn't been the easiest road, but I'm thankful for all the hills and valleys that I have had to travel to get to where I am today. I only obtained the friendly disposition I have by going through the trials and tribulations I have had to go through.

I now have a blessed life with my husband and our five kids. I'm currently in my late 30s. My husband and I both work full-time jobs and pastor an inner-city church in Killeen, Texas. He works for the school district as a P.E. Teacher, Coach, and Athletic Director. I am an executive administrative assistant for a counseling and consulting company.

Many of you may only know me as my life is now, but my story started out very differently. I want to share my story because I don't want people to think that everyone—or anyone—that attends church is perfect. Everyone has a past. Everyone goes through things, but unfortunately, not a lot want to talk about it. I wanted to completely open myself up and let people know that no matter how bad things are, there is a God who can turn it all around.

I made a lot of mistakes and put myself in so many careless circumstances as a teenager and young adult. For a while, I tried to block out a lot of what happened, but as time went on God started a new level of healing in my soul that required me to look back at where He brought me from.

I have talked to my kids about my life, and I've shared my story with several friends, but it's time for me to share the power of God and to talk about the realities of the depths He is able to deliver us from.

As a young teen, I didn't feel the love I desired from my parents, so I turned to guys for the attention. I didn't know a lot about God or that I could turn to Him for love. I put up with a lot of mistreatment in the name of "love." The first act of violence happened when I was raped at age thirteen. After that, everything began to spiral downward.

I sought love from people who were so broken they would never have the capacity to love me. I am a survivor of years of domestic violence. I was exposed to violence as a child, and then I became involved in a relationship with a violent young man. I spent years with who I thought was my first love, Edward. In reality, he both physically and emotionally abused me, and that is not love.

I've come a long way since handing my life to the Lord, and I want to share my story to give hope to others who may be facing a similar situation. There are many people in our city, and in our country, who live with domestic violence every day. Some choose to remain in their situations because they can't see a way out. For others, violence is normal; it's all they've ever known.

When I was in the middle of the worst of the violence, I believed I deserved it. But I didn't. And neither does anyone else.

This book is my life on paper. I've experienced everything I've written, and some I didn't share.

I hope you never have to experience violence as I have. If domestic violence is far from your life, there are parts of my story that may be difficult to read but read it anyway.

As you read, imagine how you would have felt in my situation. Ask God to give you His compassion and understanding for the people in your life who are trapped in what feels like a hopeless situation. Have grace for them when they choose to remain there. Pray for them to be empowered to leave.

Perhaps you have lived a similar story to mine and relate all too well. Allow the Lord to infuse your life with His strength and power. He has overcome every situation; there is no place so dark that His light cannot touch. Allow Him to guide and direct your steps toward the blessed life He has for you. No matter how you feel right now, with Jesus your life can be full of joy and peace.

One thing I ask is that you continue to read this book until the end. If you start to read the book and never finish, you will miss out on reading about the many miracles of God and how He transforms lives into walking testimonies. He has shaped and molded each of us in a way that is unique to make us who He wants us to be. I have not been the same since the day I came in contact with Him. He remade me.

# CHAPTER 1

# Early Home Life

## ISAIAH 41:10

So do not fear, for I am with you: do not be dismayed,
for I am your God. I will strengthen you and help you:
I will uphold you with my righteous right hand.

When I hear children describe their home life as "boring," it makes me cringe. Parents that have morals and standards often don't create the drama I grew up with. They might think it's dull, but at least they know what they are coming home to. For me, coming home was always a surprise and never a good one.

I was born in Indiana but grew up mostly in Copperas Cove, Texas—a small town just outside of Fort Hood and Killeen. I'm the youngest of four daughters. As a child, I was the good girl, though my sisters may not agree. It seemed my sisters were the ones that made choices that led to spankings. They were in trouble a lot more than I was. They would steal Mom's credit cards, throw wild parties, and were very popular with the guys at school. I would go out of my way to please the adults in my life.

I've always feared confrontation and physical conflict. I never wanted to disappoint my parents. I don't think I ever received a spanking—even when I deserved one. I think my fear of conflict developed due to my mom and dad constantly arguing. I hated when my parents didn't get along. There were times the arguments would become physically violent. My dad was so angry; he turned into a man that did not resemble the dad I knew at all. As a young girl, I would hide away somewhere until I knew the fight was over and things were calm again.

At one point, Dad threatened Mom with a gun. We lived in Schulenburg, Texas, and I was very young, but I still remember that night. What started off as a date night and going to a local festival, ended up as one of the scariest nights of my childhood. I remember hearing a lot of commotion and seeing my mom with a gun held to her head. My sisters filled me in on the details of that night that they remembered clearly.

When my parents returned home from the festival, my dad was carrying my mom's limp body into the house. My oldest sister, Renee, hid us in the closet to protect us from everything going on. They had gotten into a fight and accused each other of cheating. My mom hit my dad, and he hit her back. Of course, his hit did a lot more damage. My dad was drunk and playing Russian Roulette with my mom when he dragged her into the bedroom making threats to kill her.

My oldest sister took off in the car and found a police officer down the street. She led him back to the house to help mom and warned him that Dad had a gun. It wasn't long before the police were all over our front yard.

My dad took the gun with him to talk to the police. They disarmed him and arrested him that night, but my mom didn't press charges and he was released the next day. I remember Mom's face was swollen and bruised for days.

Not every memory of my parents together was a bad one. There were times when they would dance in the kitchen together and my dad would sing Elvis songs and other love songs to my mom. Dad has always had such a great singing voice. I remember those moments, like many others, so vividly even though many years have passed.

One time, my mom dyed her hair and it turned black. Normally, she was a blonde. She was crying in the bathroom and refused to come out. My dad told her she always looked beautiful, no matter what color her hair was.

I'm not sure what caused the rage my Dad felt sometimes, or what would ever make him want to hurt my mom. I'm sure it had a lot to do with alcohol because when he was sober, he was the best dad a girl could hope for. People may say that alcohol doesn't change a person, but I have seen firsthand the effects that alcohol can have.

My parents married and divorced each other twice over the course of my childhood. They weren't faithful to each other and I think the unforgiveness they had toward each other fueled arguments. Their divorce was traumatizing to me. I was torn between parents, did not know what to do, how to feel, or who to talk to. I went through the trauma of divorce twice and was even more lost the second time around. Imagine having your hopes raised and your world put back together, then having it torn apart again.

They divorced the second time when I was about 11 or 12-years-old. After that, my dad lived in the Houston area and built two companies. Mom lived in Copperas Cove, as she had two sisters that lived nearby.

There was plenty of drama around, to say the least. My sisters had made some enemies at the junior high school due to dating outside of their race. One day, some girls showed up on our lawn and told me that if I went to their junior high, they were going to make sure I was beaten every day. They said white girls had no business dating "their" young black men. I never told anyone about that incident, but I was so afraid of those girls I told my mom I wanted to live with my dad in Houston.

She was curious about why I would want to go, but she also knew I loved my dad. Though I was "Mommy's Angel," I would always be "Daddy's Baby Girl." I never understood why those girls were so upset with me, or why they would want to beat up someone they didn't even know. I just knew that if I didn't want to get my face pounded every day, I'd better leave.

My Dad was living in Pearland, Texas where he ran two successful business—one repairing liquid nitrogen vessels, and the other a drilling company. Moving to Pearland was a big transition from where I grew up in Copperas Cove. I enjoyed having my dad all to myself and life was good for a while.

I was about twelve and was responsible for all the cooking and cleaning around the house while dad was working. He bought me a horse and I loved to ride her everyday. Her name was Miss-Chuck-A-Lot, but I called her Missy. She was an Arabian Race Horse. I would ride her through the field and allow my mind to run away from everything stressful in my life.

"How come you don't ever run with her?" Dad asked me one day.

"I am running with her."

"No, that is a trot. Kick her slightly with your heel twice and she'll run."

When I did that, she took off so fast! I felt like I only had time to blink, and we were back where started from on the other side of the field. I never knew a horse could run so fast! Riding her was amazing. It made me forget that my mom and dad weren't together anymore. I felt free and relaxed like there were no troubles in the world.

When I came home from school, my bus stop happened to be by the local bar. My dad would often be there drinking and playing pool. The bartender would make me a Shirley Temple and I would play pool or do my homework. It never really dawned on me just how much my dad drank. It was a way of life that seemed normal.

Some days, I came home and there would be a couple women in the hot tub with my dad—all with alcoholic drinks in their hands. Dad's lady friends were always super nice to me. I don't know if they really liked me, or if they just wanted to impress my dad. Either way, they were all friendly.

My dad did married again. My step-mom had a young daughter that moved in with us. I honestly didn't care too much for sharing all my stuff, especially my go-cart. The go-cart was rigged so that if you wanted to use the brake you had to pull a rope. My step-sister wouldn't stop bugging me about wanting to ride my go-cart, so I let her ride it. I may not have told her about the rope. She ran into the fence and my dad gave me that look parents give their kids when they know you did something wrong, but they still found it funny. The marriage lasted about two months and they divorced.

I guess my parents missed each other and wanted to try again, so my mom came to live with my dad and brought my sisters. Things were okay for a little while, and I enjoyed having them all there. They would drink together all the time, but they didn't seem to fight as much.

I used to go with my mom to her friend Jeannie's house and babysit her little girl while they would drink. One night my mom had a bit too much to drink and was swerving as she drove on the way home. A state trooper pulled her over and asked if she had been drinking. Of course, she had! She couldn't deny it, so she told him the truth. He asked how old I was and if I knew how to drive.

"I'm 12, and yes, I can drive."

"I need you to get your mom home safely, okay?" He said.

I drove my mom home that night, very slowly and carefully.

My life was never without drama. I knew my parents still fought, and I could tell my mom wasn't happy, but I was glad she was there. I never knew what would be going on when I came back home after school or from hanging out with friends. I didn't like the uncertainty of not knowing what kind of emotional environment I was about to walk into.

One day, it was my mom's birthday. When I came home, there was a male stripper in our living room dancing as my mom sat in a chair. I couldn't believe what I was seeing!

"It's for your mom's birthday!" My dad said.

I remember turning beet red and going to my room, after laughing at my mom of course. She looked more embarrassed than I was.

I was in high school when Mom told me she was going to visit her aunt in Colorado. She called me once she arrived.

"Shannon, I'm not going to be coming back. I can't live there with your dad anymore. I am not happy. You can come to stay with me if you would like."

"What about school?" I asked. My heart felt crushed that she had just left me like that. I decided to stay with my dad. I had to make decisions that kids my age shouldn't have had to make. I didn't like choosing between my parents.

For the most part, my life became sort of normal, or I guess what I considered normal. Dad wasn't paying attention to what I was doing, so I did whatever I wanted. I was athletic and played basketball all of the time. I was good enough to play full court ball with the guys at the park. I was one of only two girls who could actually play well.

I had three best friends at school and we hung out all the time. We were very popular even though we were only freshman. Those were good and happy times.

In Colorado, my mom was dating someone and made a whole new life. She had a job and really seemed happy. I missed her so much though. The man that she was dating seemed nice as well. I was happy for her but desperately wanted her in Texas with me. There were things I needed her for. I had so many questions, and I didn't want to ask my dad anything, especially about boys.

I remember when I asked how to know if it was the right time to be with a boy. He said, "If it feels good, do it. I'm pretty sure he was either drunk or joking now that I look back on it, but I was serious when I asked the question.

## Reflection

Looking back on that stage of my life from where I am now, I sometimes wonder how it would have been if my parents had stayed together. I know they loved each other, but I also know there was a lot of bad history between them, which seemed impossible to move past.

I don't blame my mom for leaving. I missed her like crazy, but I understand her wanting to have a better life, and the urgency she felt to get out of the situation with my dad. I hated seeing either one of my parents unhappy. I can still picture my dad looking so lost in thought and lonely.

As parents, I believe Mom and Dad did the best they knew how to do. They may have not made the best choices; however, they loved us and cared for us. As my husband likes to say, parenting does not come with an instruction manual.

I recently told my parents about some of the choices I made as a teenager. They said they had no idea. I take full responsibility for the decisions I made, and I don't blame my parents at all.

I have seen such strength in my mom, and such willpower and determination in my dad since those years long ago. I love my parents dearly and have a good relationship with them both. They are not the same people they used to be, and I can call them anytime and talk about life with them. I couldn't ask for anything more!

# CHAPTER 2

# The Stage was Set

PSALM 118:6

The Lord is on my side; I will not fear:
what can man do unto me?

I was in junior high and school let out for summer. I had a few close friends I hung out with, and I would stay over at their houses sometimes. One of those friends was named Amanda. She would always be talking to cute boys on the phone.

One day she said, "I have a guy I want you to meet. His name is Giovanni." Little did I know that meeting Giovanni was going to change my world, and not for the best.

I was only thirteen, but everyone thought I was older. Most guessed I was seventeen. I wore a size eight and was fully developed, with dirty blond hair. I was beautiful and appealing, especially to a lot of older guys.

Giovanni was seventeen or eighteen. He was already out of high school but still lived with his mom in an apartment. I thought he was so cute and couldn't believe he wanted to talk to me! He would call me on the phone and always asked me to hang out with him.

I asked my sister's boyfriend to drive me to "my friend's house," which was 15-20 minutes away from where I lived. My sister's boyfriend had no idea I was going to meet a guy.

Giovanni and I would hang out in the living room watching TV and go swimming at the apartment pool. His mom was always there, but sometimes she would go to bed early. I don't think she realized I was only thirteen-years-old. My parents had no clue where I was or what I was doing.

One day, Giovanni and I were watching TV after his mom had gone to her room. He came to sit next to me and started touching me. Before I knew what was happening, he was on top of me. I started crying. He slapped me and told me to be quiet.

His act of violence somehow felt normal to me; I don't know if was because of the violence I had seen between my dad and mom, or if I just didn't know anything about healthy relationships. I thought this must be what relationships are like.

Like many people, we often relate the relationships we are in, to the relationships that we have seen. My relationship with Giovanni seemed normal from what I had grown up around with my parents. I quieted down after he slapped me. Then, he raped me. I was too scared to say or do anything to stop him. After I went home that day, I thought what happened was all my fault. I didn't tell anyone. Not a single soul.

I did go back to see Giovanni a few more times after that. Why? Maybe I was longing for love, something that was real, something I could feel, or maybe I had convinced myself that what had happened didn't really play out as it did. Though I went to see him, I never would go back into the apartment; we went swimming instead. He was angry that I wouldn't go back to his apartment with him. As we swam, Giovanni grabbed me and held me under the water. I thought I was going to die. I never went back to see him again after that.

I was 15 when I experienced my dad's drunken anger hurled toward me for the first time. I was babysitting my two-year-old nephew, Chris. Dad was drinking, of course. He stood next to a tall mirror with a black wood frame looking at me from across the room.

"Give me your mom's phone number, and her boyfriend's!" He demanded.

"No," I said calmly. "I don't want to give them to you because all you are going to do is fight."

He picked up the mirror and threw it toward the wall where I was sitting. Shards of broken glass flew in every direction. I picked up Chris, retreated to the corner of my bedroom, and called my sisters.

"Dad is drunk and throwing things," I said.

My sister drove to the house and came to my bedroom window. I passed Chris out to her. I started to climb out of the window too.

"No, you stay here," Teresa said. "You'll be okay. Dad won't hurt you."

My eyes widened with abandonment and fright.

Teresa had never let me down, and she knew Dad better than anyone else knew him, but what she said didn't ease any of my fears. I didn't know he wouldn't hurt me. I didn't have a lock on my bedroom door, and he seemed so angry.

After they left without me, every few minutes I would step out of my bedroom door and peek around the corner into the living room. Dad was passed out on the couch snoring. It was the first time Dad was ever violent toward me, and I couldn't sleep. I was afraid he was going to come back into my room. I never had that kind of fear toward my dad before. He had always been so nice to me, but I couldn't get the look he gave me out of my mind. It was as if I had betrayed him for not giving him the phone numbers he asked for.

Mom called after the incident with the mirror. "Why don't you come and stay with me in Colorado for a while?"

Another decision to make at an early age. I decided to go.

Colorado was beautiful, however, the teens that I made friends with weren't that great. They would sneak around with friends at all hours of the night and smoke weed. I wasn't interested in doing drugs, but I did sneak out at night just to hang out.

I found a part-time summer job as a waitress at an arcade and pool hall. They didn't serve alcohol, but I was around all kinds of guys there. One customer looked like a young Brad Pitt.

"Hey, do you want to try X?" One of the guys asked, offering me drugs. "It's just a little piece of paper you put on your tongue."

I tried it, but nothing happened.

Mom called me from work to see if I needed a ride home.

"No, I'm going to stay the night with a friend," I lied. I didn't even have any set plans. I just told her that so she wouldn't expect me to come home.

The "Brad" look-a-like had a motorcycle and asked me if I wanted a ride. I hopped on behind him after work and we headed to his house with some other friends. That wasn't the last time I lied to my mom and stayed out all night.

Another time, a friend from school and I told our moms we were staying at each other's houses—then we stayed out all night at the park with her boyfriend and some other guys. We talked all night and eventually fell asleep on the slides. It was cold and the next morning my body was sore from shivering all night long.

I have no idea what possessed me to lie to my mom during that phase of my life. Thankfully, nothing bad happened—we just hung out—but all the choices we make in life end up setting the stage for the rest of our lives. Looking back, I think about all the terrible things that could have happened to me but didn't. Maybe God had his hand on me even back then.

School was about to start, and I was still living with Mom. She planned to register me for school in Colorado the next semester, but Dad started calling me frequently and telling me how much he loved and missed me. He never talked to me like that when I was living with him. He told me he was lonely and that he would buy me a stereo system when I came back to live with him. I felt what he was really saying was that he was sorry for how he treated me. My family has never really been good at apologizing.

I still wasn't sure I wanted to go back to live with him. Mom tried to stay neutral about it, so I could make my own decision. Another decision.

I did miss Dad and believed he would never yell or throw things at me again. I told my mom I wanted to move back to Texas with my dad. Once I moved home, things went back to the way they always were. Dad continued to drink, and I never did see that stereo.

I made three friends at school and stuck with them. Iliana was Puerto Rican, Shameka and Ayana were black, and I was the white girl. Ayana always loved to sing; she grew up to be a radio talk show host. At school, I was friendly to other people, but my friends and I didn't let anyone come between us. We were very close.

I continued to live with my dad, and my older sisters ended up moving in for a while. Sometimes they lived with us, and sometimes they lived with their boyfriends.

Dad's businesses were doing really well, and he sometimes would have to stay up all night to finish projects. He started doing cocaine to have the energy to stay awake when he worked all night. Eventually, the guy he was buying from suggested Dad should start selling drugs, so he did—buying his product directly from Columbia.

For the most part, I was oblivious to what was going on in my house. At sixteen, I guess you would say I was sort of naïve, even though I had experienced a lot for my age. My dad, my two middle sisters, and their boyfriends would all hang out in my dad's work trailer. I thought they were drinking, but later I found out they were doing cocaine together.

My life didn't even seem real to me anymore. Who were these people? Where did my family go? I missed my sisters playing around with me and my parents—my real parents before alcohol and drugs took over their lives.

## Reflection

I would not be where I am today if it weren't for all the things I went through. Actually, none of us would be who we are without going through difficulties. That is why it is important we allow ourselves to stay in a place where we are bitter and upset about the things we have gone through. It is in those trying times that God shapes and makes us into who He needs us to be.

Even with all the terrible things we put ourselves through, our choices eventually lead us where we need to be. We learn and grow through every choice that we make. Of course, we can make our paths a lot easier if we choose more carefully, and if we try to listen to people that work hard to love us and look out for us.

# CHAPTER 3

# It Begins

ROMANS 8:25
But if we hope for what we do not yet have,
we wait for it with patience.

One of my sisters had a boyfriend that was in a Hispanic gang called Hastings. They all had an "H" burned into their arms. The guys would come over to the house a lot, and my dad started using them for side jobs—I never knew what he actually paid them to do.

The more involved Dad became with drugs, the more various people started coming in and out of our house at all times of the night—both men and women. Dad started keeping the living room TV turned to Rated R movies, and sometimes porn. He also started buying really nice cars, like a 65 Corvette Stingray, and big screen TVs. It was as if our home wasn't a home anymore, but a hangout for anyone wanting to party or get high.

When I turned 16, my sisters decide they want to throw me a party for my birthday. Well, they needed money to do that, so they used my mom's credit cards, bought plenty of alcohol, and invited a bunch of people from my school, some I had never even met before. At my 16-year-old birthday party, I drank alcohol and became drunk for the first time.

I remember being drunk. I wanted to say something so badly in my head, but I couldn't get the words out. It was as if I was trapped in my mind. I didn't care for the loss of control over my own body and mind alcohol caused. After that, I didn't drink unless there was a big party. Then, if someone challenged me, I would prove to them I could handle my liquor.

There was one girl there that always gave me a hard time. One of my sisters convinced us to have a drink off to settle our issues. I will never forget just how easy it was to drink all of that alcohol while the other girl was throwing up. I had such a high tolerance for drinking it honestly scared me. I realized I didn't like being in that drunken state of mind. I felt as if I were watching everything around me, but there wasn't much else I could do. I sat down because I didn't want to lose my balance. I stayed quiet because I couldn't get the words out exactly how I would want to say them.

Dad and I had a Rottweiler dog that had puppies, and we decided to sell them. One of the guys in the Hastings gang saw the puppies and came over to take a look at them. He was super cute, and I had never seen him around before.

"Hey, are those for sale?" He asked pointing to the puppies.

"Yeah, do you want one?"

"How about if I decide to get one, I'll give you a call—that way I can buy the puppy from you," he said with a flirtatious smile.

I gave him my number.

His name was Edward, and he called me, but not to buy a puppy. We started talking a lot—sometimes all-night long. He started coming over to the house with my sisters and the other guys to hang out and drink. He became what I considered a stable boyfriend. I was happy dating Edward. I started hanging out with him and the other gang members at the house where my sister and her two kids lived.

One night, I was with my sister and her kids waiting for the guys to come back from a party when my sister's boyfriend walked into the house covered in blood.

"What happened?" I asked. "Where is Peewee?" That is what everyone called Edward.

"I'm so sorry. I'm so sorry," the guy kept saying. "He is at the hospital. It's not good. It's not good."

My sister took me to the hospital to see Edward. Though we had already been dating for a couple of months, I had only met one of his brothers. When I walked into the hospital room, Edward's whole family was there. They looked at me, their faces asking the question, "Who is she, and what is she doing here?"

His brother introduced me, "This is Peewee's girlfriend."

One of his aunts and his grandma were very sweet toward me. They took me to the side to tell me what happened.

"They have him in surgery right now. The vehicle flipped, and they said part of his neck was broken."

I started crying.

"It's okay. Let's just wait and see what happens."

Thankfully, Edward was okay. He was alive, and that is what mattered the most to me. After the surgery, he had to wear a metal halo with screws to stabilize his head and neck.

After the accident, I noticed a complete and instant change in him. His self-image immediately dropped. I think it meant something to him that I stayed with him even though he was wearing the halo.

"He's going to need a lot of care," the doctor explained. "Edward could barely move, much less clean his own body."

"Well, he is 18 . . ." His mother said nervously.

"Shannon can help," Edward suggested.

So, I did. I would come to his house and help take care of him.

During all that was going on with Edward's recovery, I had a school assignment to pick a song that meant something to me. I had to play the song in front of the class and explain why it meant so much to me. I picked a song about a guy and his girlfriend who were in a car accident. The song was called "Last Kiss," written by Wayne Cochrane in 1961, and recorded and released nationally in 1964 by J. Frank Wilson and the Cavaliers. The song meant a lot to me because Edward could have been gone, but he wasn't—he was still there with me.

Everyone was shocked that Edward survived the accident. The car was totaled, and with his neck broken, it was a miracle he was okay.

As he continued to recover, I remember going with him to different events he liked, often Tejano concerts. I remember walking through the crowd with him and his halo.

"Man, look at him," someone said. "He's a monster— Frankenstein."

Edward wasn't used to anyone putting him down because he had looked so good all of his life. Now he had this thing on his head, and everyone was making fun of him. It really impacted his ego.

"It's okay, Baby. Just ignore them," I would say.

Before his accident, Edward would go to parties and wouldn't invite me, but after the accident, he realized his one-night stands weren't there for him. Everything he went through was a wakeup call, and it was what drew us close together in the beginning.

It had never really occurred to me until later how much of my time I actually spent with Edward. I didn't hang out with my friends much at all anymore, though I really missed them. Edward would always stress how much he needed me and how much he missed me while I was at school. I felt bad leaving his side for anything at all.

The growing distance between my family and friends and I made a huge impact on my life in the years to come, but I had no way of knowing the danger I was in at that time. I thought Edward and I were in love. I was only sixteen and thought I had found the one I was meant to be with forever. I had the life I had always dreamed of, but it would soon turn into a nightmare I wouldn't be able to awaken from.

## Reflection

I was so young and naïve then at that time in my life. Looking back now, I know there is still a part of me that always looks for the best in people and tries to not focus on their faults and failures. That's the way I've always been, and I am thankful for the way God made me because it helps me to forgive those who have wronged me and hurt me in the deepest of ways.

There is a danger in blind forgiveness and acceptance without healthy boundaries and loving oneself. I looked past all of the red flags and dangerous situations and continued to put myself in compromising situations that could have cost me my life.

Through everything I have been through I have learned about true forgiveness, but I have also learned from my mistakes. Now I know if someone does not have good intentions and is only out to hurt me or my family, I distance myself from them as fast as possible.

It doesn't mean I don't love them, pray for them, or forgive them. It just means God has given me the wisdom to stay away from toxic people. There are some family members and old friends that became very toxic over the years. I have had to distance myself from them, though it wasn't easy. I've learned that God will lead and direct me in every way I will allow Him to. He will give me the wisdom to handle even the toughest of situations, to do it with humility, and to not be haughty about it.

If we allow God to be part of our lives, He can be a strong tower when we need it, and still be the ultimate comforter at the same time. He is our counselor and friend who leads us into all truth and wants the best for our lives. He is everything we will ever need and so much more.

# CHAPTER 4

# The Monster

1 CORINTHIANS 13:4
Love is patient and kind: love does not envy or boast:
it is not arrogant or rude. It does not insist on its own way:
it is not irritable or resentful . . .

I was sixteen, and up to that point had never had a "real" relationship. Before Edward, guys just used me and moved on. It was different with Edward. We never actually developed a friendship. We went straight into dating and a physical relationship.

At that time, I drove myself to school in an '85 Trans-Am without tags or an inspection sticker. I don't know where Dad got that car, but it was mine and I enjoyed driving it. Edward didn't have a car.

"Hey, do you mind if I use your car?" He asked. From then on, he started dropping me off and picking me up from school.

One day, Edward saw me talking to some of the guys at school as he waited in line to pick me up.

"Who are those guys, and why are you talking to them?" He asked once I got into the car.

"They are just friends from school."

Eduardo and Victor were class clowns. They hung out with me and my friends—Iliana, Shameka, and Ayana—and were always trying to make us laugh.

"I don't like you talking to those guys," Edward said.

The next day at school, my friends asked why my guy was glaring at them so much.

"He doesn't like me talking to you," I explained.

"Oh, you need to break up with that guy!" Eduardo said.

But I didn't. Instead, I started distancing myself from my friends. I would do anything to please Edward. I even started distancing myself from my girlfriends.

One of my biggest regrets is that I never told my friends the truth about what happened with Edward. To continue being with him, I had to cut off all ties with my friends. They were such good friends. I hate that I just left them like that. I tried to reconnect with them about five years ago, but it was as if we were strangers. The choices I made so long ago had lasting repercussions. I am still in contact with Iliana and Shameka; we text occasionally.

I didn't pick up on Edward's jealousy as being a red flag or as being controlling. I was wrapped up in the attention he gave me, which was a nice distraction from life with my dad's alcoholism and drug use.

The situation with my dad continued to escalate. He was constantly doing drugs. The Rottweiler puppies had fleas, and our house became infested. It was horrible. Our house was in complete chaos and my dad didn't seem to notice at all.

"I can't believe you are living like this," Edward said when he was at our house one day. "I want you to move in with me. I will talk to my parents."

Edward's parents considered themselves strong Catholics, even though they didn't go to church. He was 18 and still lived with them. They weren't crazy about the idea of their son's girlfriend moving in.

"You guys need to do this right and get married," his dad said. I was only 16.

"Oh, we will," Edward said. "This is just temporary."

"Okay," they relented, and I moved in with Edward at his parent's house. When I moved in with Edward, my Dad didn't even notice I was gone for about a week or so.

The first week I lived there, I started joking around with Edward. His reaction was so funny I started laughing. I was just playing around, but he didn't take it well.

"Why are you laughing at me? Stop laughing at me."

I continued to laugh, and he reached over and slapped me.

I was so shocked, I just kept laughing.

"Why are you still laughing? I just slapped you."

"I am shocked that I just got hit by a guy," I said, a little dumbfounded.

"What did you expect?"

That was the first time Edward hit me. I had heard stories of how his dad would hit his mom, so I guess his family was used to it. I never saw his dad hit his mom. Edward told me that once when his mom was pregnant, his dad threw her out of a moving truck, and she miscarried their baby.

I learned that as Edward and his brothers grew older, they would stand up for their mother. There were three boys, and all of them grew to be bigger than their dad—except for Edward. He was my height and 150 pounds, which earned him his nickname—Peewee.

After that first incident where Edward hit me, I began to watch what I said around him. Eventually, I learned it didn't matter what I said. If he was in a bad mood, he would take it out on me. If his parents heard Edward doing something to me, they would just say, "Stop, Edward." They never actually did anything to stop the abuse or protect me.

Most of the time, his family would keep quiet, and back out of the way. Every once in a while, his mother would say, "Stop doing that. You're going to end up just like your father."

One day we were lounging around the house and then decided to go to a flea market. I started getting ready and putting on make-up.

"You haven't worn make-up all day," Edward said. "Why are you putting it on now?"

"Well, we are going out. I don't like to go out without make-up on."

WHACK!

He slapped me really hard in the back of the head. He never hit me directly on my face because he didn't want to leave marks that anyone could see. He would hit me on the back of my head, or on my arms or body, so I could cover up the marks.

"You haven't worn make-up all day. You're going to look pretty for everyone else, but you can't look pretty for me?"

That was his logic.

We finished getting ready and loaded up in the car. The flea market was filled with nearly all Hispanic people. Edward was really good looking, and he was with me—a white girl. The Hispanic girls would look at him, then look at me with a look on their face that asked, "What are you doing with her?"

Edward would look back at them and flash his big smile.

"Are you looking at them and smiling?" I asked.

"Yeah. What are you going to do? Nothing."

Edward was right. There was nothing I could do. We had reached the point in our relationship that I had no say in anything. It was pointless for me to open my mouth and say anything—it would only result in him hitting me.

That was the day I realized I didn't matter, that I meant nothing to Edward. I realized I wasn't worth him being faithful to me. Our relationship started going downhill from there, but it wasn't close to ending.

Edward had already told me I would never be able to have a guy better than him. I had seen what my parents' relationship was like, and I had never been in another "real" relationship with any other guy, so I thought maybe he was right. Plus, Edward was extremely good looking. I began to have a feeling of worthlessness, a feeling of "this is it."

Maybe he is right. Maybe I am worth nothing. Maybe this is the best I'm going to do in life.

Before I had gotten with Edward, I had been very promiscuous, sleeping around with many guys, but I hadn't been faithful to any particular one. I just went along with whatever the guy I was around wanted to do. I told myself I was living in the moment.

Now I was in a relationship with Edward, and I was faithful to him. I didn't look at or think about any other guys. I did love him—at least it was puppy love. In some shape or form, I loved the monster.

I don't know if I was afraid of him or not. I know I wanted to make him happy, so he would never hit me again. I didn't want to do anything that would cause him to hit me again. I didn't want to make him angry. I never wanted him to lash out at me again. I don't know if I was full of the fear of disappointing him, or if I was afraid of making him angry.

One time, we went to a party for one of his family members, and Edward gave me permission to drink with him. I had a margarita and a daiquiri, but they kind of snuck up on me and I zoned out. My eyes were still open, but it was as if I was asleep.

I watched as one of Edward's guy cousins talked.

"Are you serious?" Edward said, looking at me with fury in his eyes.

"What?"

"You're staring at my cousin."

"He's talking. I'm watching him talk."

"Come outside with me now!" We went outside to the parking lot.

"What are you doing staring at him like that?"

"I had a lot to drink. I'm just here. I'm not thinking of anything."

Edward grabbed me by the back of my hair and shoved my head into the window of a nearby car. It didn't break the window, but I remember my head throbbing and throbbing. I didn't say anything else.

We walked inside and sat back down. I wiped away my tears and put my head down on the table. I didn't want to be accused of staring at someone else again.

One of Edward's female cousins came up to me concerned. "Are you okay?" She asked.

I nodded my head, "Yes." I didn't want to get in trouble for saying anything else.

# Reflection

There is no way to ever know in advance if someone is going to hurt you or cause you harm. We must listen to the still small voice of truth inside that lets us know something is not right. Too often, we dismiss that voice. That is what I did with Edward. The voice of truth was telling me there is something really wrong, but I wanted to believe otherwise.

If you are ever in danger, get out. I can honestly say from experience that abuse is not love. Don't wait around as long as I did and risk your life on a chance that things might get better. God has so much more in store for you, and He does not want any of us to be in pain or live a life of fear. Fear is not of God.

Looking back, I know I missed all my family tremendously during that phase of our relationship, but out of fear I never contacted them to tell them what was going on, what I was actually going through on a day to day basis.

My oldest sister, Renee had moved out long before I was a teenager. She was much older than me and moved out at 18. She had joined the Air Force and became a nurse. Though she wasn't there for much of my life, I know she loved me dearly and would have done anything to keep me safe.

My sister Teresa was back in Copperas Cove. She had a great job and was doing well for herself. Teresa was my protector and always looked out for me. Out of all my sisters, these were the two I always knew I could count on to be there for me. But I couldn't bring myself to tell them what was happening, not yet.

# CHAPTER 5

# Trapped

PSALM 34:18
The LORD is close to the brokenhearted
and saves those who are crushed in spirit.

Whenever Edward was mad or angry, he would scream at me and called me names. When he yelled at me like that, I didn't want to be alive anymore. I didn't feel like I was worth anything.

"Maybe you would be better off if I was dead," I would say.

"Well, then go ahead and do it then," He responded.

There were two different times I tried to kill myself in front of Edward. I wanted him to feel guilty and to have to live with my death for the rest of my life.

"You've hurt me for the last time," I yelled. "I'm leaving." I grabbed the car keys and headed for the front door.

Edward grabbed the keys from me, but I ended up getting them back from him. I unlocked the car, and then threw the keys into a field next to the house. I climbed into the car and locked myself in. It was triple digits in the Houston summer, and the car was hot.

I'm not sure exactly why I threw the keys, I think I wanted him to feel helpless while I slowly died in front of him. Maybe a part of me wanted him to look for the keys and rescue me.

At first, Edward began yelling and banging on the car window for me to get out. "Fine. If you want to do that, stay in there!" He went back into the house.

I stayed in the car for a couple of hours. I wanted to inflict more pain on him than he had on me. I didn't care if I died. I started pouring sweat. No matter how hot it was I was determined to stay in the car.

Edward would come back outside every once in a while, to check on me.

"I'm sorry! I'm sorry! Please open the door. If you don't open the door, I am going to bust open the window. I love you."

After what seemed like an eternity, I finally relented. I was burning hot, dripping sweat, and I felt so weak. I opened the door and climbed out of the car. As we walked inside, he started in on me.

"You are so stupid. Don't ever do that again." He started hitting me as soon as we walked through the front door.

How stupid of me to think he would actually care if I died. He was more concerned with his image. He didn't want the neighbors knowing we were not the perfect couple he told everyone we were. We weren't perfect, to say the least. We fought all of the time. Edward's violence continued to escalate, and I continued to accept it.

It wasn't long after that, Edward blew out the engine in my Trans Am. My Dad said he would get it fixed for me, so he had it towed. I knew it wasn't going to be fixed and that it would probably just be sold. Dad had an Eclipse he wasn't driving, so we bought the car from my dad, and faithfully paid on it. We were one payment away from paying it off, and the next day,

Dad had one of his employees come and steal the car! I went to see him about it.

"Dad, I can't believe you did that. Where's the car at? We were about to pay it off!"

Dad was sitting at his desk with crack laid out in front of him.

"Get out! Get out of my sight! Don't come back!"

It was difficult seeing my dad like that. He wasn't himself when he was on drugs. He was looking at me, but he had a blank stare in his eyes. It's almost as if he wasn't in his body anymore. He completely dismissed me from his presence. He was full of shame. I don't know if it was shame from me confronting him about stealing the car the night before, or from me walking into his office and seeing him for who he had become.

Moving back in with Dad was not an option for me, and besides that, I loved Edward. I was faithful to him, and I would put up with anything to stay with him. No matter how much he hurt me.

I came out of Dad's office and climbed into the car we borrowed from Edward's family. Edward was looking and waiting for a response. I started crying and said, "We aren't getting the car back. I'm sorry. My Dad is on something and won't even talk to me."

During those days, I would babysit my niece a lot—so much to the point that people thought she was mine. Once when I had her at the house, Edward became mad at me and grabbed a knife. I don't even remember what we were fighting over.

His explosive temper always took over, even when we were fighting about stupid stuff. There were times he would beat me up if his food was in the pan instead of on the plate. Why would anyone beat up or kill another person over something like that?

I grabbed Victoria. She was not even two at the time, and I loved her very much.

*I can't let anything happen to her.* I thought. *It can happen to me, but not to her.* I grabbed the baby and got in the car, taking her back to my sister's house.

While I was gone, I worried Edward was going to hurt himself. I called him to see if he was okay.

"I didn't mean it, Shannon. I wasn't really going to hurt you. I would never do that."

I dropped my niece off at my sister's as if nothing happened and went straight back to Edward. I still struggled with thoughts of suicide, particularly after bad fights with Edward. Once, I tried to tell him how I was feeling.

"Sometimes I want to kill myself because I don't matter to you. What's the point of living? I am just going to kill myself," I said.

"You keep saying that and you keep talking. Why don't you just go ahead and do it?" He said handing me a knife.

I took the knife from him and pulled it up into the air as if I was going to stab my wrist. He reached out right before the blade made contact with my wrist and grabbed the knife by the blade, nearly severing two of his fingers. He ran out of the room holding his bloody hand.

His brothers heard a commotion and ran in from the other part of the house.

"What's going on?" they asked.

"I was doing dishes and cut my hand," Edward lied.

They took him to the ER to have his hand sewed up. His nerves were severed, and the doctors were trying to piece him back together.

I felt horrible like it was all my fault. I was the one who hurt him.

"Shannon, what really happened?" Edward's brother asked.

I told him.

"He is so stupid sometimes."

The man pitied me for a second, but he treated his girlfriend the exact same way Edward treated me.

As Edward's hand healed, he realized he suffered some permanent damage. For years, he had played the bajo-sexto, a Spanish guitar. They would pay him to play for gigs and various concerts. With the damage to his hand, Edward couldn't play the guitar anymore. He worked through the pain to force his fingers to work again. He was so angry.

"This is all your fault. You did this on purpose," he said to me. He never took any responsibility for his own actions. It was my fault he was hurt. It was my fault he brought me the knife, my fault he egged me on, and my fault he grabbed the blade.

## *Reflection*

With all of the terrible things that happened back then, I look back and can see the grace and mercy of God—not only in my life but in my dad's life as well. When I remember the hurtful things Dad said and did back then I know it was the drugs and alcohol influencing him. My dad never meant to hurt me or say things to break my heart. He was a wounded, hurting person.

It would be years before our relationship would mend, but it eventually did. I held on to the hurt for far too long. It wasn't until after God showed me love and forgiveness that I was able to show it to others.

Eventually, my dad prayed for God to deliver him from drugs. He started reading the Bible and praying. God delivered Dad instantly from drugs. As far as I'm aware, he did not attend rehab or a 12-step program. God just instantly delivered him.

God has a way of mending even the most broken people and restoring them to be even better than they were before. My dad started going to church with me for a while. He received the Holy Ghost and was baptized in Jesus' Name!

Dad and I now get along better than we ever have before. We can call one another and share what God has done and how good He has been. Only God can restore relationships in that miraculous way!

# CHAPTER 6

# *Babies & Bruises*

DEUTERONOMY 31:6
Be strong and courageous. Do not be afraid or
terrified because of them, for the Lord your God
goes with you; He will never leave you nor forsake you.

Less than a year after I moved in with Edward, I found out I was pregnant. I was sixteen, and I was so excited! *"He won't hit me while I'm pregnant,"* I thought.

I thought Edward would value me as the mother of his child and begin to really love me. I thought his outlook on us would change to mean so much more than me just being the girl that lived with him.

I was wrong. His outlook didn't change. Edward didn't hit my stomach when I was pregnant, but he still hit me everywhere else especially in the head, just not the face. He didn't want the abuse to be obvious.

I felt hopeless. *"He might change where he hits me, but he is still going to hit me,"* I realized.

When it came time for me to give birth, Edward was out drinking with some of his friends. His family told him I was in labor and he showed up to the hospital completely drunk.

In a way, he was excited to be a father. He was proud to have a son. He was also proud that we named him after him—Edward James the Second. I didn't want to name my son "Junior" because

I didn't want him to be a miniature Edward, but I did like the name.

I turned seventeen, and still, I had a lot to learn as a new mom. I didn't go to any kind of parenting class, so I was pretty much on my own to figure things out. Edward would hold the baby and play with him, but he refused to change diapers or feed him. He never took responsibility for our son's care.

I stayed home almost all of the time. The only place I went was the grocery store, and, if I took too much time there, Edward would accuse me of sleeping with other guys.

A couple of weeks after baby Edward was born, he began to cry in the middle of the night. Edward was furious.

"If you don't get him to shut up, I'm going to hit you."

"He's going to be okay. Just give me a few minutes." I had to do everything in the dark. Diaper changing, feeding, and comforting the baby. Edward did not want the light to bother him.

"I'm going to count down, and even if you're still holding him when I get to one, I'm going to hit you! 10, 9, 8, 7, 6, 5, 4, 3 . . ."

The whole time Edward was counting down, I was rocking the baby. When Edward got to three, I realized my little one was not going to stop crying. I kissed him on the head and laid him down. I closed my eyes and braced myself for the attack.

"1!"

He went straight for my face—an uppercut to my lip. Blood came pouring down as my lip busted wide open.

He hit me so hard he cut his knuckle on my teeth. He looked down at all the blood. "I'm sorry. I'm so sorry," he said.

In some sort of sick penance for what he had done, Edward picked up a miniature souvenir baseball bat he had from the Houston Astros. It was a wooden bat, about a fourth of the size of a regular bat. He started hitting himself in the head saying, "I'm so stupid. I'm sorry."

He kept hitting himself as if he were waiting for me to stop him, but I didn't want to. Part of me thought, *This is what he gets. I'm not going to stop him from hurting himself.*

"Stop, Edward," I finally said.

He didn't have blood pouring down his face as I did, but I felt bad about how he was hurting himself. He laid back down on the bed and passed out.

The next morning, there was a city parade marching on the street behind the house where we lived. I put a hat on and pulled it down low to cover the marks on my face. I stepped out of the house to take baby Edward to watch as the people passed by. When I returned Edward wasn't happy.

"Where were you?"

"I was at the parade."

"What are you doing just taking off like that?"

He took my head and pushed it into the sliding glass door. I remember a loud boom as I hit the glass. My head was throbbing.

His mom was in the living room watching the whole thing and yelled at him to stop. He took off to the bedroom.

Every once in a while, Edward's mom would say something about the violence, but sometimes she just ignored it. I wouldn't call her a loving, doting grandmother either, but on occasion, she would help me feed and change the baby.

I remember one time when baby Edward was crying as he fought going to sleep. I was lying next to him trying to get him to go to sleep. Edward's mother barged into the room.

"What are you doing to him? That's not a normal cry."

"He's just fighting sleep. I'm not doing anything to him."

"Just wait, I'm going to tell Edward when he gets home!"

I could never win.

The baby was about a year old when I found out I was pregnant again. I was about two and a half months along when Edward punched me in the stomach. I was actually driving on the highway at the time and Edward was mad about something.

I started crying and holding my stomach.

"Nothing happened. You're fine," he said. "You are just paranoid. If you hadn't made me so mad, this wouldn't have happened."

After that, my stomach didn't feel normal. Two days later, I started cramping really bad. I took a shower hoping it would help. When I looked down, there was blood everywhere. I passed an oval-shaped clot. I wrapped it in tissue and put it in the trash, thinking it was just a blood clot.

I did go to the hospital. The nurse asked me to describe what I had passed. I told her. She asked what I did with what I had passed. She used an ultrasound to confirm I had miscarried.

I felt so horrible after I found out that little clot was my baby and I had put it in the trash.

"Don't worry, you can still get pregnant. You can have more children."

Her statement made me angry. The baby had just died, and the nurse was already trying to replace the child. She wasn't giving me a chance to grieve.

The nurse did not ask me what happened to cause the miscarriage, so I didn't tell them about Edward hitting me. They assumed I miscarried from natural causes.

Edward was quiet when I told him I lost the baby. He never said he was sorry and didn't take responsibility for what he did.

It wasn't long after that, and I became pregnant again. Edward was excited and hoped it was a boy. Unfortunately, being a dad didn't inspire him to want to be a better person. He still went out and partied all the time. He didn't change at all. We still lived with his parents. Edward was not motivated to get a place for us.

After I had my second son, Noah, we finally moved into our own apartment. Edward started working with his brother at a company in Pasadena and smelled like fumes from all the chemicals he was working with. He made good money, and we lived in a cheap apartment, but we still lived paycheck to paycheck because Edward would blow it all on alcohol and drugs.

One morning, I heard a tow truck beeping in the parking lot and looked out the window. They were repossessing our black Trans Am. Edward hadn't been making the payments.

After that, we briefly had a Mustang. I didn't get attached to our cars because Edward was constantly driving drunk, crashing and totaling vehicles. He totaled at least two of our vehicles. I have no clue how we continued getting approved to purchase new cars.

After the car was repossessed, there was a period of time where Edward was on his own for the first time. He was paying all the bills, and his parents were not there to help take the pressure off.

Our apartment was directly above where the landlord lived. One day, Edward pushed me, and I fell hard on the floor. The woman from downstairs came up to check to see if everything was okay.

"Yes, everything is fine," I said after answering the door.

"Are you sure?"

"Yes."

I closed the door.

"It's a good thing you said that," Edward said. "Or else things would get worse for you."

A couple of months later, I went downstairs to pay the rent.

"Come on inside while I write your receipt," the woman said.

As I walked into her apartment, I realized I could hear everything that was happening upstairs, every footstep.

*"There is no way these people don't know that he beats me,"* I thought. Still, no one had called the police. Here were people that obviously knew what was happening, and no one was doing anything about it. Just like Edward's parents, the couple turned their heads and ignored what was happening to me. I felt alone like no one cared. I just wanted someone to reach out to me.

I was so young back then. I didn't realize I was a victim. Edward had distanced me from all friends and family. He was all I had, and it felt like nothing I ever said would ever matter to anyone.

## Reflection

Sometimes in our lives we just need one person to care, just one person to let us know that we matter to someone and are loved. I so desperately needed that while I was going through this terrible time in my life, yet there was no one. No one that I could see, anyway.

I now know God had His loving arms around me even back then. While I was separated from my family and friends, He never left me. He gave me the strength to make it through and He helped me make it from day to day. I didn't know Him as I do now, but He has always known me.

Though there have been times over the years that I have felt alone, I know He is always with me. Sometimes, it is just the enemy that wants us to think we are alone. He knows that if we believe we are alone, he can defeat us more easily.

There is strength in numbers. Though at times I still feel alone and defeated, I believe there is an angelic army ready to fight on my behalf because God loves me that much! The wonderful thing is that He loves us all that much! There is not one of us that God would not go to battle for.

CHAPTER 7

# *Leaving Psychoville*

JEREMIAH 29:11
For I know the thoughts I think toward you,
saith the Lord, thoughts of peace, and not of evil,
to give you an expected end.

At this point in our "relationship," Edward and I had three boys, little Edward, Noah, and Joey. The boys and I would sleep in the bed together most nights because Edward wouldn't be home until the morning anyway. Our family shared a mobile home with Edward's brother and his family.

He and his brother would go out and party most nights. Edward no longer cared enough to hide his adultery. He went to the clubs several times a week and would return covered in lipstick and smelling like perfume.

"What's that?" I asked pointing to the lipstick.

He looked down and flipped his head back, "Yeah, so?"

I realized he was completely, 100 percent using me. He was blatantly sleeping with other girls, and still expecting me to take care of him, the kids, and the house.

I knew I didn't love him anymore. Whatever good I had seen in him was no longer there. I decided I didn't want to live my life with him using me anymore. I didn't even want him to touch me. He disgusted me.

When he would start to make a move, I would push him away. "I'm sorry; I don't love you like that anymore." He would become angry, throw a fit of rage, and rape me.

It was Christmas of 2001. I had spent the previous six years wishing Edward would marry me. When I finally let go of that idea, he gave me a ring for Christmas. I wasn't even excited about it. I could see the disappointment on his face at my reaction to the ring. He must have realized he was losing me, but he didn't do anything to change his behavior or to win me back.

My third son, Joey, was about 5-months-old when I made up my mind; I was leaving Edward. I just had to figure out how to leave. I was 21-years-old and had lived with Edward for six years. I began to slowly, secretly pack things in a suitcase, which I kept hidden at the back of the closet.

Edward was getting ready to go out and party when I asked him if it was okay if I went to visit my sister Teresa.

"Why?" He wanted to know.

"I haven't seen her in a while," I said. "I just miss her."

He hit me on the side of the head with his fist and I fell to the floor.

"You're not going. If I let you go, I know you won't come back."

"Yes, I would come back!" I tried to convince him.

"If you ever think you are going to leave me, our boys will grow up without a mother," he threatened.

I was still lying on the floor where he had knocked me down. He started kicking me with his steel-toed work boots.

Four-year-old Edward came over to me and said, "Daddy, Daddy stop! You're hurting Mommy."

He pushed little Edward away and he fell to the ground.

"Oh, God, help. God, help!" I cried.

"Not even God can save you from me," Edward said as he continued to kick me.

Seeing little Edward on the floor beside me was the moment I knew I was leaving. I didn't want my sons to see me hurting like this. I didn't want them to be victims of Edward's abuse as well.

Edward stopped kicking me and went to the bathroom. I pulled myself up off the floor and sat on the edge of the bed. *"Tonight is the night,"* I thought. *"I'm getting my boys and taking them out of this situation and lifestyle."*

It was about 8:30 p.m. and Edward and his brother were getting ready to head out to the club. He was combing his hair and dressing up. He put on his cologne—Safari. The smell still gives me flashbacks of that horrible season of my life.

"Don't even think about trying to go anywhere," he said as he started out the door.

I said, "Okay. I'm not going anywhere. I'm staying."

He left, and I waited for the car to finish going down the driveway. I looked out the window to make sure he was gone then started pulling out everything I had packed out from the closet. I added photo albums and some of the boys' clothes into the suitcase.

Something told me to look out the window again. It was a good thing I did! Edward's car was racing back down the driveway to the house!

I threw the suitcases back into the closet and covered them up again. I sat back down on the bed just like I was before he left, trying not to breathe too heavily.

He stood in the doorway of the bedroom and looked at me. "I just want to make sure you weren't stupid enough to try anything." Then he left again.

This time, I waited about 10 minutes after he left the driveway, and I once again slowly started taking everything back out of the closet.

Who would I call? I hadn't planned that part. I decided to call my sister, Teresa, who lived about four hours away in Copperas Cove.

"He's been hitting me for the past six years. I need to get out tonight." I told her everything that happened that night.

"Shannon, I had no idea," she said. I'm going to call Renee. I'll call you right back." Renee was our other sister who lived in Houston about 25 minutes from me.

Renee called me. "I can't believe you are going through this. I'm on my way. Just wait by the door."

Edward's brother's girlfriend was still in the house. His brother would hit her too, but she would hit him back.

"I can't believe you are finally getting out," she said. "I wish I could go too."

"You can."

"No, I can't. I can't leave," she said.

"Okay, well I'm leaving anyway." I knew there was nothing I could say or do to change her mind. She had to be ready to leave for herself.

Renee pulled her suburban into the driveway. I piled my kids and all our stuff into the vehicle. Part of me still felt bad for Edward, so I went back into the trailer and left a photo album of the boys' pictures there for him. Then we took off.

Renee drove us to Teresa's house in Copperas Cove.

"How do you feel?" Teresa asked when I arrived. "Do you have any regrets about leaving?"

"No. I finally feel free for the first time in years. I don't see how anyone would want to go back to that."

"Do you love him?"

"I stopped loving him a long time ago."

I didn't tell the boys we were not ever going home. "We are going to visit your Aunt Teresa," I explained.

The next day Noah, who was two, asked, "Where's Daddy?"

Little Edward remembered what had happened the night before, and he didn't ask about his dad.

"We are staying at Aunt Teresa's house for right now," I told Noah.

The weirdest thing about the situation was how quiet it was. A part of me expected Edward to drive the four hours to us, storm down the door, and beat me to death.

It was two days before Edward called. He sounded quiet and sad on the phone.

"I just want to see the boys. I miss them already. It's fine if you want to stay there. I just want to see them for a few hours. Maybe they can stay the night with me and then go back to live with you."

He sounded sincere, and I felt guilty for just leaving, but I wanted to make sure he was for real. I waited about two weeks to see if his attitude changed, or if he started threatening me. He never did.

Teresa and I planned a trip to take the boys to see their dad. She stayed with me the whole time and we met Edward in a public place to drop off the kids off. As we drove away, I had a sinking feeling that something wasn't right.

I called to check on the boys, but Edward wouldn't let them talk to me. After a couple of days, I realized he wasn't planning to bring the boys back.

I called him. "We need to schedule a pick-up."

"Yeah, they are not coming back."

I realized I was going to have to trick him to get the boys back, just like he tricked me to take them away. I decided to lie to him.

"I really regret leaving you, Edward. I want to be a family again. I just need to bring them back to Copperas Cove because they have doctor's appointments. After that, I'll bring them back and we will be a family again."

I couldn't believe it, but he bought the story!

Teresa and I drove to Edward's house to pick up the boys. I knew he was observing me, trying to find out if I was playing him. I told Teresa to take the boys to the car, and I stayed in the house by myself with Edward.

I walked up to him. "I really love you and miss you. I can't wait to come back," I said. Then I kissed him for a long time. Kissing him sickened me, but I knew I had to make him believe me, and that did it.

I climbed into the car with my sister, shut the door. As we pulled away, I said, "Leaving Psychoville. Population 1."

"You're such a nerd," she said. She still teases me about saying that.

We went back to Copperas Cove with Teresa and ended up living with her for the next several months. At first, I had no idea what to do with myself. I had a lot of problems to work through, and I had no idea how to start.

I didn't think I was depressed, but at the same time, I didn't feel I was the best mother for my children. I thought they would be better off with my sister, or someone who was a stronger person than I was. I felt weak, discarded, and worthless.

Little Edward would check on me when I was looking sad or spaced out. He was used to checking on me, so it was something he still did. "Mommy are you okay?" he asked.

Noah, on the other hand, started becoming bitter. He didn't understand why he couldn't see his father. He was still a toddler, but he would become angry, and started calling me a "B." That was what Edward taught him my name was. It was difficult dealing with his tantrums, and it didn't help me feel like a good mother.

I knew I needed a change in my life. It was time for me to step up and find a job. My sister had a friend who worked at a call center. I applied for a job and got an interview. They hired me, and I started working full-time.

The boys would go to daycare or Teresa would watch them for me while I worked. She had two kids of her own, and I would watch them for her as well. It worked out perfectly because we had alternate work schedules. Her boyfriend also lived in the house, and he was supportive too. It was a good start for our new life.

## Reflection

After I left Edward, I thought everything would be great all the time. I would no longer be abused. Life would become happy again. Looking back, I realize I was so consumed with my problems that I missed the fact that my other family members were going through a lot during this same time.

My Dad lost everything and had. The IRS seized everything—the house, properties, and cars. He had to overcome his addiction, which, as I mentioned earlier, was only by the grace of God. He was pretty much alone during that time. I know my sisters would try to help him, but he was also pushing a lot of people away.

My sisters had children I barely knew because I had isolated from my family for so long. My Mom had remarried a great man named Glenn, and even though we stayed in contact some, we had a lot of catching up to do. I wanted us to all grow close again. I wanted us to put all the past hurt aside, and just be a family again.

I made contact with my dad for the first time in years. We talked and apologized to each other. I was so sorry for leaving him when he needed me the most, and he said he was sorry for not being the dad he wished he would have been. He still doesn't remember most of the things that he said or did, but none of that matters. What matters now is that we have pushed through what would have destroyed most families. We have chosen to love and forgive.

CHAPTER 8

# A Call Center, A Club, & A Church

ROMANS 8:38-39
For I am persuaded, that neither death, nor life,
nor angels, nor principalities, nor powers, nor things present,
nor things to come, nor height, nor depth, nor any other
creature, shall be able to separate us from the love of God,
which is in Christ Jesus our Lord.

I worked at GC Services, a customer service call center. I started gaining self-confidence through work and the friends I made there. We took phone calls for a bank and answered questions concerning people's accounts. It was a fun place to work.

I had one particular girl there that I was friends with—Sandy. She was a bit heavier than my size 8 frame, had blonde hair, blue eyes, and was always smiling. She had her tongue pierced and seemed to have so much self-esteem. I enjoyed hanging out with her and noticed that she helped me to have fun and build my confidence.

"Why don't you go out with your friends after work?" Teresa asked me one day.

I had never been a partier. I was faithful to Edward for all six years and mostly stayed home during that time.

Sandy was always inviting me to go out with her. "Come to the club with me! We will dance and have fun!" She loved country music and seemed to really enjoy her life. I decided to go clubbing with her.

At the club, guys started buying me drinks and asking me to dance. I wasn't used to that much attention, and I kind of went overboard. I started off going to the clubs with Sandy one or two nights a week. That quickly turned into five to six nights a week.

I was drinking every night, staying out until 4 a.m., coming home, showering, getting a couple of hours sleep, and going to work. I continued partying like that for nearly a year.

At the call center, our team leader was a guy named Jason. He was friendly with everyone, always joking around. He was like the class clown, just at work, and we always had fun. We could transfer our calls to him if the customer wasn't happy.

I don't think Jason caught onto it, but a lot of girls would flirt with him. He was a good looking, six-foot-tall, black guy. His dad had been in the military, and he had traveled a bit growing up. He was born in Kansas, had lived in Germany, and his dad ended up retiring in Copperas Cove near Fort Hood. He had a great personality and was a lot of fun.

I never flirted with him; we were just friends. We smiled and laughed together, and I'd tell him stories of what happened the night before at the clubs.

Our team all got along, but occasionally we made fun of Jason because he would always invite us to church. Jason had never drunk alcohol or done drugs in his life. He was kind of sheltered. Outside of work, everything else was about church for him. He was the kind of guy who kept in contact with his friends from high school.

It wasn't long before I started dating a man I met at a club. His name was James. He was a bull rider, very good looking, and had a strong southern accent. He was about my height and had a sort of strong, rough look to him—he once broke his nose bull riding. He was definitely a cowboy, through and through. He was in the Army and stationed at Fort Hood.

When the girls at work saw me with James, they swooned. "Oh, my goodness!"

He seemed to be the opposite of Edward in every way. When he saw me at the club, he bought me a drink and asked me to dance. We dated for about three months. During that time, he kept asking to meet the kids.

"I'm not ready for you to meet the kids," I said.

I came home from work one day to find James at my house with presents for my kids. He took it upon himself to meet them without me. He brought them a baseball and a bat. My sister had let him in; she didn't know I wasn't ready for him to meet the kids yet. I was not happy.

"We need to take a break," I said to James. "I wasn't ready for you to meet the kids yet. This is going way too fast."

The next day, he had flowers delivered to me flowers at work.

When the delivery person came through the door, Jason looked over at me and busted out laughing.

I read the card. "I'm sorry. I love you. I want things to work."

After my shift was over, I went outside and found James there waiting for me.

"We are supposed to be taking it slow," I said.

"I know; I went overboard. I shouldn't have gone to the house. I shouldn't have met the kids."

I accepted his apology and kept going to the club with him. It wasn't long before James received military orders to move to Hawaii. He wanted me to go with him and proposed we get married. I had only known him for three months!

"I'm sorry," I said. "I'm not there in my life yet. I'm not ready to get married. I think it is better if we don't see each other anymore."

The next day after work, I arrived home and James' truck was outside. He was inside the house again, sitting on the couch, upset. My sister, Teresa, was consoling him.

"We need to talk," I said with my arms crossed.

"I'll just give you guys some space," Teresa said. The look in her eyes whispered to me on her way out of the room, *I can't believe this guy is here crying!*

"We can't do this," I said. "You need to find someone else. You're a great looking guy. I know there is someone else perfect for you out there."

A few days later, I was back at the club with my friend, Sandy. Another guy asked me to dance. I looked around to make sure I didn't see James. He wasn't there, so I accepted the invitation.

As we began to dance, something flew past me from the other side of the room. It was James. All of a sudden, the guy I was dancing with flew across the dance floor. He was on the ground. I don't know if James punched him or pushed him, but the guy was down, and James was standing over him. The guy stood up ready to fight.

Sandy and I rushed over, stood between them, and tried to calm them down. We were able to prevent the fight.

The next day at work, I told Jason what happened. He busted out laughing. "That's hilarious! You sure know how to pick 'em!"

Jason never stopped inviting me to church. He would joke with me when I came in to work with a hangover. "Well, you know, if you didn't drink, your head wouldn't be pounding today."

I eventually decided to counter his offer. "If I go to church with you, then you have to go to the club with me," I said. I had never been a regular churchgoer. Growing up, we went to a Baptist church on Easter and Christmas.

He started laughing. "That's not happening," he said.

One week, Jason told me about a Kid's Power Hour at his church. It was a special event with puppets and fun music.

"Okay, I'll take the kids to that," I said.

I didn't have a car at that time, so Jason picked us up and took us to church. When I walked into the church with the boys, the people were very nice and welcoming. I wasn't used to people being that friendly. They could see I was a single mom with three kids, and it didn't bother them at all. Being a single parent, I expected some kind of judgment, but I only felt love. The preacher was lighthearted and funny. I enjoyed the service and told Jason I liked it.

"Well, if you enjoyed it, you should come back," he said.

I wasn't so sure about it, but I had a good time, so why not.

## *Reflections*

I didn't expect to feel such a huge amount of love from such a small church. I didn't know then that the pastor and his wife would become such a huge part of my life. They were so genuine with the love they showed, and I was not used to that.

I had so much anger and hatred bottled up; I didn't even know I was holding on to all the negative emotions. People actually cared for and loved me. Not because I was a fun drunk or they could get something from me, but just for who I was as a person.

In that season of my life, I was at a fork in the road. I knew that whatever choice I made could change everything. I could either keep going the way I was going, putting on a fake smile while completely hating myself and my life, or I could see what this whole Pentecostal church thing was about, and what would happen if I kept going.

# CHAPTER 9

# A New Kind of Drunk

ACTS 2:17
And it shall come to pass in the last days, saith God,
I will pour out my Spirit upon all flesh . . .

I started going to church with Jason on Sunday mornings. A few services later, I started added Sunday nights. Jason continued to pick up me and the boys.

"Why don't you come on Wednesday nights too?" Jason asked.

"You guys have church all the time!" I said. A couple of months later, I started going on Wednesday nights as well.

I introduced Jason to Teresa when he came to pick us up for church. She decided he was a nice guy and a funny friend. After a while, some of the young people from the church started coming over to hang out at the house. Teresa didn't mind. She thought everyone was really nice and fun to be around.

Even though I started going to church, I was still going out to the clubs. I had to back off on partying and bring it down to three nights a week at the club instead of five. After all, I was going to church on Sundays and Wednesdays, and if I was hungover on Sunday morning, Jason would make fun of me. I decided I enjoyed going to church more than to the club, so I stopped partying on Saturday nights.

Despite going to church, I still felt the need to drink all of the time. I would drown myself in alcohol. I still felt as if my boys would be better off without me, so I would drink to try to forget everything that had happened. I drank every day for at least eight months. It was the first time in my life I was drinking on a daily basis.

Looking back, I can see it was a period of depression. Part of me just wanted to end it all. I had suicidal thoughts off and on. I would think about the best way to leave my kids with my sister. I would drink to try to leave the problems behind. Even when church friends were at the house, I would sneak downstairs and drink alcohol. I hid it from them, but I was completely dependent.

When I started going to church social events—like the Christmas banquet—it was nice, but there was no alcohol. I watched everyone having fun and playing games. They were a lot of good people having fun together like a family. The experience was an eye-opener.

"This is a family," I thought. "If you have all these people around you, you have the love of a family. You don't need alcohol. You just need each other."

I had lived in Copperas Cove for about a year and a half and had been going to church for about six months. I was very reserved at church. I don't like to be out in front of people and have them looking at me. I was hesitant about going up to the altar to pray with everyone else at the end of services. If I did pray, I would stay in my seat and pray. No one would even know.

It was mid-December, and I felt a tug on my heart to go to the altar.

Sister Knight, my pastor's wife, came up to me at the altar. "Do you want the Holy Ghost?" She asked.

"Yes," I said. I had learned about the Holy Ghost at a Bible study and I knew I needed to be filled with God's Spirit.

"You have to repent so that Jesus can fill you with His Spirit. Do you know what it means to repent?" she asked.

She explained that repentance wasn't just asking for forgiveness from sin, but it was completely leaving the behaviors behind. I went to the altar, knelt down, and I repented from my sins. I ended up standing with my hands raised in surrender to God. My arms were feeling tired, but my body felt like it was on fire. There was an energy all around me that I couldn't explain.

Two church friends, Christina and Sister Cuevas, stood on either side of me, praying with me. When I felt the most tired, I raised my hands a little higher and started thanking God for forgiving me, and all He had done in my life. I felt a wave of God's love wash over me, and I started speaking in a language I had never learned before.

It was the same experience I heard happened in the Bible in the book of Acts, where one hundred and twenty believers were filled with the Holy Ghost on the day of Pentecost. The Bible tells the story that some people thought the believers who were speaking in tongues were drunk because they were acting emotional and different from the normally acceptable behavior.

When I received the Holy Ghost, I felt a surge of positive energy. It was a supernatural experience. I felt changed. I felt cleansed and free. I knew my life would never be the same from that point on. I had perfect peace inside of me and trusted that God had everything under control.

About a week after I received the Holy Ghost, I decided to be baptized in Jesus' Name. I knew it was important to be baptized, but I thought it was more symbolic than anything. As I stood up out of the baptistry, I had the feeling that I was leaving my past in the water.

Between receiving the Holy Ghost and being baptized in Jesus' Name, it felt like every horrible thing I'd ever done and that had ever happened to me was gone. I was a new creation in Christ. The guilt I felt about being a horrible mother left. I walked out of that service dependent on Jesus. I was ready to live the new life He had given me.

It wasn't long before I had to make a choice to continue living for God in my daily life, outside of the church, and outside of a strong emotional experience.

My friend from work, Sandy, had a birthday coming up. I promised her I would go out with her to the clubs for her birthday, but I really did not want to go.

"I just got the Holy Ghost and got baptized," I explained to her. "I don't really want to go."

"You have to! You promised!" she said. I gave in.

Once we arrived at the club, she told me I had to drink. I drank one sip, but it didn't taste good. It didn't taste the same way it used to. I didn't want it. All I wanted was to drink from the well of life—the Spirit of the living God.

A guy came up beside me and said, "You look like you are really out of your element here."

"Yeah," I said. "I started going to church. I feel like I shouldn't be here."

"Oh, yeah? What church do you go to?" he asked.

"Copperas Cove United Pentecostal Church."

"Oh, yeah? I'm Pentecostal too," he said.

It didn't seem right to me that two people who knew God would meet up in a bar. I knew that people who lived for God didn't go out to the clubs. I knew if I was going to live for God, that I had to leave.

"I've got to get out of here," I said to the guy, and stood up to find Sandy.

"Look, I'm sorry, but I have to go," I said to my friend. "I can't stay. I don't feel comfortable here anymore."

Sandy wasn't happy with me, but she said she understood. After that, Sandy didn't think I was fun anymore and didn't want to hang out with me.

After my friendship with Sandy dissolved, I stopped going to the clubs and started spending time with my kids. They loved spending time with me and doing things together. From that point on, everything changed. The kids stopped asking about their dad. Their whole outlook on life began to change, and so did mine.

## Reflection

Many of the friends I had before I found the Lord did not end up staying around. A lot of them may not have understood my new walk with God, or the changes I made in my life. I had lost some friends before becoming a Christian, but this time the process was different. In coming to God, I had gained a whole church family in the process.

I could talk to my pastor and pastor's wife about anything and they would not judge me at all. They always gave me good advice and backed it up with scripture. They loved me and prayed for me often. I knew that I had made the right choice and I knew God was with me the whole time.

Sometimes, I would think about the night I left Edward. His words echoed in my head, *"Not even God can save you from me . . ."*

But God already did!

CHAPTER 10

# A New Beginning

PROVERBS 8:35
For whoso findeth me findeth life,
and shall obtain favour of the Lord.

As the weeks went by, I kept attending church and became very involved in church activities. I had joined the choir and even began working in the nursery and Sunday School. In what spare time I had, between work and church, I hung out with my friends from church, which included Jason.

When New Year's Eve rolled around, I had everyone over to the house. I cooked a big breakfast to celebrate and bring in the New Year. We had a great time laughing, joking around and just enjoying being together.

Everyone started to leave, and soon it was just Jason and me left. We went to say our goodbyes and noticed the mistletoe hanging above our heads. Jokingly, we started laughing. Then, suddenly, something changed.

I looked at him in a completely different way. He was no longer my goofy, nerdy, friend from work, Jason. He was a godly young man who had a sincere love for God, and who was very handsome.

We kissed.

It all became clear to me now. God had placed us together. He knew I never wanted to date again and that I didn't trust men, so He placed a perfect gentleman in my life who would lead me to God. Nothing would ever be the same.

Jason and I began dating and were inseparable. We were already friends and my boys knew him well. They were thrilled when Jason came over. He would build forts for them in the backyard and play games with them. He was such an amazing boyfriend.

I often felt that because of my past, I would never be good enough for him. He assured me that he had prayed for someone like me, and God answered his prayer. I was so thankful God brought us together.

I had rented my own house and moved out of my sister's place. My dad gave me a car and things were going great. For the first time ever, I was independent. It felt so amazing to be paying my bills on my own, cooking for my kids, and cleaning my own house.

Jason would come over after work to have dinner with us and hang out a bit before going home. Sometimes Jason would take my house key and clean my whole house while I was at work so that when I got off, I wouldn't have to do anything. He was everything I had ever wanted in a boyfriend.

During that happy season, I hadn't given much thought to Edward. Then one day I received a court notice in the mail. I had to go to a custody hearing and meet with him face-to-face. Though I knew I would be safe, and we would be meeting in a courtroom, my stomach still dropped.

I shared my anxiety with Pastor Knight. He told me I was a child of God now and I had nothing to fear, but that he would be there at the court to support me. I couldn't believe that my pastor cared enough to drive all the way to support me at the court hearing. He cared so much to be there for me like that. It meant the world to me that I didn't have to face Edward alone.

When I arrived at the courthouse Pastor Knight was there, but Edward never showed. The court issued a warrant for his arrest because he failed to appear in court, and they said they would reschedule the hearing for a later date. I thanked Pastor Knight and told him how much him being there meant to me. He reassured me that everything was going to be just fine. He was so sure it would all work out for the best. I longed to have that kind of faith.

I began attending Bible studies with Sister Knight, the pastor's wife. I just loved spending time with her. She was always so wise and the kindest person I had ever met. She had such a sweet and selfless personality. I knew she was like that because of her relationship with God. I always looked up to her and hoped to be like her one day. When I told her about my fear of Edward, she said sometimes we have to pray for God to "remove the mountains from our life." She said, sometimes people can be mountains too.

I knew that I and my boys were not safe as long as Edward was in our lives. I began to pray for God to remove that mountain from us. I had since dedicated the boys to God at church and would pray for protection from anything that would harm them.

The second court date was scheduled, and again my stomach sank. Though Pastor Knight couldn't make it to the second hearing, Jason came with me so that I wouldn't have to be alone.

Edward showed up and brought one of his brothers with him. He had a look of total shock and disgust that I had brought another guy with me. I found it odd that he didn't glare at me or threaten me in any way. It was almost as if he was intimidated.

When the mediator began going through child support information, Edward began bragging about how much money he made. He didn't realize that the more money he made, the more he was going to be paying in child support.

His pride seemed to work out in my favor. When it came to the custody portion, the court wanted to give shared custody. I explained I was not comfortable with shared custody, and that Joey, my youngest didn't even know Edward as his dad. Surprisingly, Edward agreed and supervised visitation was ordered. I couldn't believe how everything was completely working out. It had to be God!

Edward started to contact me about seeing the boys. He convinced me to let them spend a weekend with him. I did feel bad for him being away from his kids and knew that he missed them. I hesitantly agreed, and we dropped them off for the weekend.

Jason was unable to go with me to pick the kids up, so my friend Ms. Sister Cuevas went with me. When we arrived at the McDonalds to get the kids, Joey was covered in ice cream. I had to take him into the bathroom to wash his face and hands. As soon as I went through the bathroom door, I heard someone behind me.

Edward pushed through the door and blocked it. He had an evil grin on his face as if to say, "Now I got you." Before I knew it, Ms. Sister Cuevas had wedged herself between Edward and me.

"Can I help you with something? I think you better leave!" she said.

Edward just responded with, "Oh, I forgot to give the boys one of their tapes." He handed me a tape and said, "I'll see you later."

I knew exactly what he meant. It was a threat. He would see me later, when no one else was around, and finish what he wanted to do to me then.

It amazed me how Ms. Sister Cuevas was not scared at all. She stood right up to Edward. I asked her how she could do that and not be afraid, knowing how he was.

"It was the Holy Ghost in me." She explained that God gives us the strength to stand up for ourselves in times when we should be scared, and that fear was not of God. I hoped and prayed for the day that I would no longer let fear rule my life.

We made it back home and I thanked my dear friend again for being there for me.

When I told Jason everything that happened, I could tell it bothered him that he wasn't there. After that, things went back to being great again. My life had some normalcy to it again, but I still had episodes of fear concerning Edward.

Sometimes I would have Jason stay on the phone with me at night because I was scared Edward was going to break into the house and finish me off. I would hear footsteps in the hall, even though I knew no one was there. One time, I thought heard whispering outside of my bedroom door. I thought I heard Edward explaining how he was going to kill me.

I peeked toward my door and saw the shadow of someone standing on the other side. I knew it wasn't real, but fear made it all seem so real. I pulled the covers over my head and called Jason. I had him stay on the phone with me until I fell asleep. I felt like I was losing my mind.

I told Pastor Knight everything that was happening, and he explained to me that fear is a spirit. He said I wasn't losing my mind, but that I was under a spiritual attack. He said he would pray for me and over my house, and that I needed to do the same. After we prayed, I never had an episode of fear like that again.

Many evenings, Jason would come over to the house and explain parts of the Bible to me. As we studied the Word, we grew closer together. As time went on, it was evident that we were meant to be.

On Valentine's Day, Jason was supposed to come over to pick up the boys and take them to his mom's house, so she could babysit while we went out to eat.

He came by the house and asked if I could drop the kids off at his mom's instead of him taking them. He said he didn't feel like going with me to his mom's. I was not very happy about that, but I begrudgingly did it anyway.

After I dropped the boys off, I walked back into my house to find my living room filled with presents. I immediately started crying. I couldn't believe Jason had done all of this for me.

He bought me a phone, perfume, and many other gifts. As the tears of joy were running down my face, he said, "I'm not done yet. I have one more gift for you."

He pulled out a ring, and I ran and hugged him. I was so overwhelmed with joy and excitement. The tears just wouldn't stop.

"Is that a yes?" he asked.

We both laughed, and I said, "Yes."

It was all so perfect and felt like a dream. We went out on our lunch date and afterward shared the good news with our friends and family. I couldn't believe how truly blessed I was.

One day, Edward called my house and Jason answered the phone. They talked for a long time. Jason thought that maybe we should give Edward another chance to see the kids for a weekend. I was confused. Jason said that Edward had apologized for everything he had done, that he meant no harm, and just wanted to see the boys and spend time with them.

We went to drop the kids off and a couple days later went back to pick them up. Jason and I both got out of the car. Edward wouldn't even make eye contact with me. He said a few goodbyes to the kids, a quick "thank you" to me, and then he left.

It dawned on me that because Jason was there, he wouldn't dare try anything. I didn't truly believe Edward was sorry, or that he had changed, but I was happy the exchange went well.

Unfortunately, as soon as we started to head home, I learned something that shattered my happiness. I learned that Edward made all the boys drink a little beer. Little Edward refused to drink it, but his father had put beer in Joey's bottle. He also taught the boys how to shoot a gun and made them shoot a rabbit. He made little Edward hide a beer behind his back in the car after a state trooper pulled Edward over.

I was furious, to say the least. My fear was gone, and I emailed Edward to tell him all the things I had discovered. "You will never have them alone again," I wrote.

He responded, writing, "Whoever told you all that is a liar."

"So, your calling little Edward a liar?!"

"No, I'm sorry. Can I just talk to him and tell him I'm sorry?"

That was the last time Edward took the boys for the weekend. He still had supervised visits, but only completed two before asking to have them alone again. I said no, and after that, he never met up with the boys for another supervised visit. He absolutely hated being told no and having someone else there for accountability.

I was going to do whatever it took to protect my boys, and I called the Attorney General's Office and told them that.

## Reflection

I never thought that a mountain could ever be removed, but God did it! I never talk bad to the boys about their dad. I always answer their questions honestly and tell them I will never lie about anything that has happened. My boys have grown up without being around drugs, alcohol, or a life full of domestic abuse. God answered my prayers and has protected all of us the whole time.

It's amazing how drastically life can change in a matter of a few years. I went from being an abused, scared mother who felt worthless and had no desire to live, to becoming a strong child of God, and a loving mother who was getting ready to marry her very own Prince Charming.

CHAPTER 11

# The Fairytale Life

SONG OF SOLOMON 6:3
I am my beloved's and my beloved is mine.

As our wedding day drew nearer, it all seemed surreal. How could I be getting married, and to such a great guy? My boys were excited too. They weren't just gaining a father, but Jason's whole family had welcomed us in.

Jason's parents went to church with his sister. I had met his entire family, even his brother who lived in the Dallas area. His parents are still together and completely love each other. His upbringing was the exact opposite of mine. It is funny, we learned we lived on the same street as kids, but we didn't know each other. We must have just barely missed each other when I moved to the Houston area. His parents had accepted me and the boys as part of their family from the beginning and had always been so welcoming to us. That is, they were welcoming after what I refer to as, "The Talk."

Jason's dad, Mr. Dorsey, had asked me to lunch one day after Jason and I started dating. We met for lunch and ordered our food. I was so nervous. I had no idea why he wanted to meet with me alone. After we ordered, there was an awkward silence, then he asked, "What are your intentions with my son?"

I was speechless, and was finally able to get out the words, "What do you mean?"

He replied, "Some people date for fun. Are you dating for fun, or with the intention of marriage as a possibility?"

I stated, "I'm a mother of three boys, and I am past dating for fun. I would not date anyone unless I had true feelings for them and saw a possibility there for marriage."

He said, "That's all I needed to hear. Welcome to the family. Let's eat."

Of course, after that conversation, my stomach was in knots. I couldn't finish my food and had to take it to go. Jason's dad gave me a big bear hug and said I handled "the talk" well and that he was happy I was part of the family. Though it was nerve-racking and a bit scary, a big relief washed over me. They didn't care that I had three boys from a previous relationship at all. They completely accepted me and my kids. His parents always treated the boys as if they were their grandchildren from the start.

My parents and I talked often. They both had remarried and moved on at this point. I was happy for both of them and they seemed to be doing so much better without being in each other's lives. Both of my parents would be coming to our wedding and both would be bringing their spouses. Part of me was a little concerned but I had a feeling it would all be alright.

My mom shipped me a few wedding dresses from Colorado, and I picked out the one I liked the best. Mr. Dorsey asked me what flowers I wanted and had me pick out a bouquet. He paid for the bouquet and the limo for the wedding.

My dad helped pay for the reception hall and the church. Mrs. Dorsey helped with all the decorations. A friend of mine was styling all of the bridesmaids' hair for that day. Of course, Pastor Knight would officiate the wedding. Everything was planned and ready to go.

The wedding day arrived. I was nervous but so excited and happy. My hair was styled, and I and met up with the bridesmaids, my mom, and my grandma at the Dorsey's house. We all got dressed there and took several photos. It all felt too good to be true, yet it was real. I was going to marry my best friend in a couple hours. Not just my best friend, but the one that led me to God and completely changed my world forever.

As we got in the car and headed to the church, little Edward looked at me and said, "When do I have to start calling Jason, Daddy?"

"I would never make you call him Daddy. That's something you decide all on your own."

He said, "What if I want to call him Daddy?"

I smiled and said, "I'm sure he would love that."

It was such a beautiful wedding and reception. It felt like it all went by so fast and was over before we even knew it. Everyone was so happy for us. I was so happy that all of our closest friends and family came to share that beautiful day with us.

Pastor Knight had warned us that not everyone would be so kind toward us as an interracial couple outside of the local military area where we lived. We soon found that out. On our way to our honeymoon, we stopped by a really nice restaurant outside of Austin. There were only a few people eating and we asked for a table for two. The hostess said there were no tables available. We inquired about a wait list and stated there were plenty of tables.

She gave us a look and said there were not any tables available for us. I knew what she meant. We were a mixed couple, and we were not welcome. It hurt so much that people could be so full of hate over something as ridiculous as the color of skin. We left and found a good place to eat down the road. We knew that we had to be careful where we went and the places that we stopped at. It was sad that people could be so ignorant. Despite that incident, we had a wonderful honeymoon and we were excited to start our life together as husband and wife.

When we returned to Copperas Cove, Jason moved his things into our house, and our lives resumed. We were one happy family. Jason told me I could stay at home with the kids for a while and take a break from work if I wanted to. So, I left my job and enjoyed being a stay-at-home mom. Jason's sister, Stephanie, would come over and we would hang out a lot. I would also babysit some of the children from church from time to time.

We had been married nearly a year, and though we had been trying to conceive, we weren't having much progress in that area. I went to a doctor who said that based on my symptoms, I could have endometriosis and that it would be unlikely that I would become pregnant. The doctor said that over half the women who have endometriosis are unable to conceive. I didn't want to believe it and kept going up for prayer at church.

There was a church ladies' conference in Lufkin that we went to every year, and I went with some friends from church. On our trip, one of the women thought for sure she was pregnant, so we all went to the store to buy her a test. It turned out negative and she was very disappointed. I felt so bad for her because I knew how she felt.

At my first church service after the ladies' conference, Sister Knight approached me.

She said, "Congratulations!"

I said, "For what?"

She smiled and said, "You're pregnant!"

I explained that we had been trying, but weren't successful and that I wasn't pregnant.

She gave me a hug and said, "I'm not asking you. I'm telling you. Congratulations, you are." She gave a big smile and walked away.

I told Jason what she said. We went straight to the store and bought a pregnancy test. Sure enough, it was positive! I am still amazed at how Sister Knight always knew things like that, but I understand it is because God fills her in. We went on to have a healthy, beautiful baby boy. We named him "Nathanael," which means "a gift from God."

Around the time Nathanael was born, my grandma was in Houston dying. I wanted so badly to see her, but there was no way I was going to be able to make it there. I remembered how she loved to come to visit the church with me and how she was always so funny. She made quilts for all her grandkids and had already made one for Nathanael. It was so tough knowing she passed away asking for me, and that I couldn't be there.

I remember crying so hard and not being able to stop. I asked God to please comfort me and to help me have some peace. It was as if He wrapped His arms around me and held me. I immediately stopped crying and had such a sense of comfort and peace at that moment. There was such a warmth on the inside as I held on to all of the good memories I had of my grandmother.

Jason and I now had four boys and had discussed adopting a girl, but we were still deciding. He said if he ever had a daughter, he wanted her name to be Miracle. When Nathanael was six months old, I went in for my check-up and routine exam.

The nurse explained that they could not do part of the exam. When I asked why, she replied, "Because you are pregnant, Mrs. Dorsey."

I was in shock and said, "No way!"

Then they showed me the results and said, "Yes, you are pregnant."

I was excited and scared. We were going to have five kids! We had tried to have an ultrasound done to find out the gender of our new baby, but in each case, they were unable to tell. We even paid for a special 3D ultrasound appointment in Round Rock, but our car broke down on the way. We had to ride in a two-seater tow truck all the way home. I was nine months pregnant, sitting on Jason's lap as the tow truck driver brought us home.

Poor Jason, he couldn't feel his legs by the time we got home. We gave up trying to find out the baby's gender and decided we would just see when the baby was born.

The day arrived, and my contractions were close enough to go to the hospital. I was in labor. Within a few hours, our daughter Miracle was born. We were so overjoyed and happy to have our little girl. We decided five was a good number, and I had the tubal ligation surgery. Our big family was complete.

# Reflection

Looking back on those days, we didn't have a lot of money, but we were so happy. There were times we would have to eat beans, rice, and cornbread for a week, but there was never a complaint. We had everything we needed, God, and each other. Sometimes I think back and miss those times, especially now that we have a lot of teenagers.

God has blessed us immensely. I have a beautiful family, a loving husband, an awesome church family, and a great relationship with my parents. I lost my grandma, but through that, I came to know God as the ultimate comforter. I had seen God as a Healer, Provider and so much more during that precious season of my life. My past was just that, my past. I was moving forward in a new life, with a whole new outlook on life.

Jason encouraged me to go back to school and get my G.E.D. and eventually my associate degree. He was always lifting me up and encouraging me in every endeavor. He went to every basketball game, soccer game, and band performance the kids had to cheer them on. He was exactly what we needed, and God knew that. Jason and I have accomplished so much in ministry, education, relationships, careers. I could go on and on, but it's all only possible because of God.

The thing that I have come to understand is that I am special in God's eyes. We all are, and anyone can decide to change their life and live for him. Anyone can accomplish great things and encourage others to do the same. Anyone can choose to not be satisfied with the status quo and aim so much higher. With God, all things are possible. I know that now.

CHAPTER 12

# Storms Will Come

PSALMS 107:29
He maketh the storm a calm,
so that the waves thereof are still.

Sometimes things can be going so well, and then life just happens. I had been working at Wal-Mart for a while on the overnight shift when I received the message. Pastor Knight had passed away. We all knew it was possible, due to some health issues he had, but when I got the message, I couldn't believe it.

I had to leave work. I needed to get out of there. I started reminiscing on all of the conversations we had over the years. Our latest talk had been a bit different. I told him what an impact he had on my life, and how I was so thankful that he was my Pastor.

He said, "Shannon, you are an inspiration to me."

That really stuck with me, because I never understood how "I" could be an inspiration to anyone, especially to Pastor Knight. It would take years later for me to finally understand what he meant.

As children of God, our main purpose in this world is lead people to God. When Pastor Knight said I inspired him, he meant that I inspired him because I was one of the lost sheep who was brought in. It was inspiring to know that the lost could be won and that you can make a difference in someone's life. It's inspiring to see someone completely transform their lives and live for God. I have no doubt that Pastor Knight helped win many, many souls, I'm just so honored and thankful that he was my Pastor and took time to help and guide me. He was such an inspiration to me, and I will never forget him.

I knew that Jason was hurting over the loss of Pastor Knight as well. Pastor Knight was his pastor for twice as long as he had been mine. Jason always looked up to him. We would often tell stories about Pastor Knight, or go through photos and videos we had, and just remember the good times. I hated not knowing what to say or do when Jason felt grieved over the loss. Sometimes, I would just hold his hand and be there.

Over the next few years, we would lose more friends that we loved so much. Our dear friends Nimala, and Sister Jennings from church passed away as well. Both were such amazing people and so full of love. They both gave so much to others. Though I didn't understand why they had to go, I had no doubt they were all going to be walking on streets of gold with our Pastor Knight.

My mom and Glenn, my step-dad, had come to live in Texas from Colorado. We enjoyed going to Colorado every year to visit them, but I was so happy they were moving closer. Now we could see more often, and the kids could spend a lot more time with them. Glenn came a few months after my mom did, and we all knew something was not right. He took longer on the drive than he normally would have.

Glenn was a tough cowboy, over 6-feet-tall. He used to drive big semi-trucks, so a 17-hour drive should have been like nothing for him, but took him two days to make it to Texas. When he arrived, he said his vision seemed off, and we all thought he was acting a little different.

My mom took Glenn to the doctor and they immediately started to run tests. The results didn't take long, and we found out that Glenn had Glioblastoma, an aggressive brain cancer. We learned that the prognosis does not have a high survival rate, and that treatment must begin immediately. My mom was heartbroken and distraught, but we were all trying to be optimistic.

Glenn was one of the toughest guys I've seen, and he was determined to beat cancer. He had to undergo brain surgery to try to remove as much of the tumor as they could. It was like waiting on pins and needles for the doctor to come out and update us. He finally came out and let us know what we feared all along; they weren't able to get all of the cancer out. They removed what they could, and Glenn would have to go through radiation and chemo to try to get rid of the remaining cancer.

At that time, I was working for a pediatric clinic as a medical biller. I was able to take off and drive my mom and Glenn to each of his radiation treatments. We would also go to Temple to see his oncologist. After every appointment, we went to a local chain restaurant called Cotton Patch Café to eat. Glenn always ordered the fried pickles as an appetizer.

After the last appointment with the oncologist, the doctor said that the tumor wasn't shrinking the way that they had hoped and that another appointment wasn't necessary. I followed the doctor out of the room and said, "Please tell me the prognosis. We need to know how long."

The doctor replied, "Two months or less," he said. "I'm sorry."

The car ride home was very quiet. I know Glenn and my mom had questions and I hated to be the one to answer them. Glenn said, "So, I don't have to go back. That's good news, right?"

I replied quietly, "No, Glenn. I'm sorry, but it's not good news."

He said, "But the doctor said he doesn't need to see me anymore, so that's good. Right?"

My mom couldn't take it any longer. "No, Glenn. He is trying to say you won't be around for your next appointment!" She burst into tears.

I knew she was brokenhearted and devastated, but Glenn's silence is what hurt the most. He understood he was dying, and there was nothing that could be said to comfort or console him at this point. We pulled up to the house and I went around to help him out of the truck. He was always insistent on doing everything on his own, but after three tries he relinquished and let me help him.

As we walked toward the house, he pulled me into one of his big bear hugs and whispered, "Thank you for everything. I love you."

"There is nothing to thank me for. We are family. I love you too," I said.

As the days went by, I would stop by their house as soon as I got off work to spend time with Glenn and Mom. Our small amount of time with him went by way too fast. I watched our strong, tall, cowboy fade away, and then he was gone.

He could make the best cabbage burgers you could ever taste and wouldn't want you to lift a finger if he was around. He loved to cook and clean up afterward because, well, no one could get it cleaner than he could. He may have had a little OCD, but we loved him for it, and we miss him so much.

His daughters and some of the family were able to come to visit him before he passed away. We were able to laugh and have a good time, which is the way he wanted us to remember him as. He wanted us to remember him for the big, strong, cowboy he was.

Jason officiated the funeral and did so well. It was such a beautiful ceremony and tribute to such a great dad. I'm thankful for the time I had with him, and will always miss his, "I love you to pieces" voice and big bear hugs.

My mom was never the same after Glenn passed away. She always had a kind of sadness there. I know she still misses him, so much. I wish there was more I could have done for her, but I know everyone must grieve in their own way.

## *Reflection*

Losing so many people that were dear to me was one of the most trying times in my life. I found strength where I didn't think I had any left to give, and I know that had to come from God. I was able to help my mom and Glenn through everything.

On the inside, I may have been a weeping, blubbering mess, but God helped me to help them the best way I could. He gave me strength when I needed it so that I could help those around me. He was my strong tower and my very present help in my time of need.

My mom is doing a lot better these days. She moved away from Texas and is now living with one of her sisters. Though I miss her, I know she needed the change, and I hear happiness in her voice now that was not there before she left. I know she still misses Glenn like crazy, but she is going to make it.

Sometimes it is in the chaos of the storm, that we find the strength in God that we need to make it through. We know that if we can survive the worst, and just make it through, then there is nothing that can keep us down.

# CHAPTER 13

# *From Comfort to Calling*

## ISAIAH 6:8
Also I heard the voice of the Lord, saying,
Whom shall I send, and who will go for us?
Then said I, Here am I; send me.

While we were dating and before Jason proposed, he said we had to have a talk. He had some serious questions to ask me. Jason was not serious very often, but when he was, it was usually pertaining to major life decisions and ministry.

"I know that I am called to preach, and one day maybe even pastor," he said. "Will you be willing to go with me anywhere God leads me?"

I replied, "Yes, Jason. I love you and if we marry, I'd be glad to go with you anywhere you're called."

I tucked that conversation into the back of my mind, and life moved on.

After we married, Jason and I stayed involved in many ministries in the church in Copperas Cove. Through the years, we both sang in the choir, taught Sunday school, served as greeters, and helped clean the church. You name it, we have done it, or helped in any way we could.

Jason served as the youth pastor for about 10 years. Throughout that time, I was right by his side. We watched our youth group triple in size. We were always raising money for them to go to special church events in the district. There would be times we would go to youth events that lasted all night. We drive home the next morning running solely on coffee. We absolutely loved every minute of it.

We saw many young people grow up to follow their calling. Some have gone on to be music artists, preachers, missionaries, and involved in many other efforts to reach the lost. When you see someone grow in God and receive His Spirit, it makes every effort and time spent giving in ministry worth it.

Long before I came along, my husband had the heart of a soul winner. Pastor Knight used to preach about being friendly, loving people, and leading them to the Lord and salvation. Winning souls was our purpose and goal in life. Jason has the perfect personality for soul-winning. He has always been a talker and could start a conversation with anyone. I take a little while to warm up; I guess you could say I'm somewhat of an introvert.

Our children, Edward, Noah, and Joey, all received the Holy Ghost there and were baptized in Jesus' Name. The Copperas Cove church was the only place our kids had attended. Nathanael and Miracle were born while we were members there. We loved our church, but we both felt God tugging on our hearts to do more. We began to pray, and God gave us several confirmations that we were about to shift into a new ministry. I kept thinking of Jason's call to be a pastor that he told me about so many years ago.

At our church district ladies' and men's conferences that year, Jason and I both received confirmation that we were meant to leave our place of comfort. God had something in store for us. Then, at a district conference, the Superintendent, Brother

Prince, said, "There is someone here who is called to a city that is 20 minutes from where you are now."

Jason and I both looked at each other. A close friend of ours had mentioned that the pastor of a church in Killeen was retiring, and that there would be an opening for a new pastor to go there. It was exactly 20 minutes between where we went to church in Copperas Cove and the church in Killeen.

After several confirmations from God, we knew it was time to go, but that it would not be easy because we loved the church where we had been for so long. They were like family to us, and we had known most of our friends there for over 15 years.

Sometimes, God makes us a bit uncomfortable as He confirms a call on our lives. Maybe the discomfort helps push us a bit when it is time to go. Whenever you decide to obey God's will, there are always going to be people that do not agree with the choice that you make. Change, even a good change, isn't always pleasant, and it isn't always supported. We still had listen to and obey God's will.

In the process of taking a step into the next chapter of our lives, some people did not agree with what we were doing and that hurt us. Even people that we trusted for a long time caused us pain. For me, it was heartbreaking because I had never seen anyone in church behave or act in such a hateful manner.

Jason reminded me that we are all flesh and blood; no one is perfect. Everyone falls and does and says things that may be hurtful to others, even if they are in church. That is where forgiveness, grace, and mercy come in.

It took me quite a while to get over my pain, but I found I could learn something from it. I learned that even in the toughest of situations, I never want to say or do anything that would cause someone to be as heartbroken as I was. I learned to always try to see things from the other person's perspective before speaking.

I tell this part of my story for two reasons. First, when I see someone making a choice that I don't necessarily agree with, it is so important for me not to be a stumbling block to them. Instead, of saying something directly to them about their choice, I choose to love, encourage, and pray for them. Secondly, not everyone is going agree with the choices I make, and many times I will have to walk the road God calls me to all by myself. But I can be encouraged! God will be with me every step of the way.

When we left, we received a lot of words of encouragement and prayers from all the church family we had known over the years. Looking back now, I know it was God's way of nudging us out the door so that we could finally begin the calling He placed on our lives so very long ago.

As we transitioned to The Lighthouse UPC in Killeen, Texas, Pastor Samuels and his beautiful wife warmly welcomed us. The congregation was much smaller than we were used to, but we knew it was our new "home church" right away.

Jason began playing music and alternating preaching with Pastor Samuels. I became involved in Sunday school and the worship team. All of our kids said they were scared about going to a new church at first, but now that we were actually there, they loved it. It's funny how when we hear of a change, we immediately start to become uncomfortable, but when the change is in God's plan everything just falls into place.

After six months of attending The Lighthouse and serving there, it was time for the church to make a decision. Voting night was coming up, just a little over a week away. We were ready and excited.

Though he doesn't get sick often, Jason hadn't been feeling well. We both didn't think much of it and wrote it off as a cold. It was New Year's Eve service and Jason was going to open the service in prayer.

The Assistant Pastor, Brother Hamilton, came up to me and asked where Jason was. I said I didn't know. "Maybe he went outside for some air; he wasn't feeling well."

A few minutes passed and Brother Hamilton rushed in and said, "I will finish out the service. You may need to take your husband to the hospital or home."

I went outside and found Jason sitting in the car. He had just thrown up, and in all my years of knowing him, I don't think he has ever thrown up. I asked if he wanted to go to the hospital.

"No, just home for some rest and I will be fine." We went home and he went straight to bed and fell fast asleep.

When morning came, I woke up and realized Jason was still sleeping. He was always awake by 5 a.m. each morning, and it was already 8 a.m. I knew he wasn't feeling well, so I thought maybe he just needed more rest.

Then it dawned on me, what if it was a lot more than that? A few years back, Jason had been diagnosed with Type II Diabetes, but was able to manage it with diet, exercise, and medication. What if what was going on had to do with his diabetes? I asked him where his testing kit was, so I can test his glucose level. He replied, "It's in the ground, outside."

I knew then that I had to get him to a hospital, and quick. I called my father-in-law and told him what was going on. He immediately headed over to our house. I had to get Jason dressed, and try to get him into the car. He couldn't stay awake long enough to do anything. Everything he said didn't make any sense at all.

When we arrived at the hospital and told them what was going on, they announced a possible "DKA status" and rushed him immediately to the back. DKA is diabetic ketoacidosis, which is a serious complication of diabetes that occurs when your body produces high levels of blood acids called ketones.

The condition develops when your body can't produce enough insulin and begins to break down fat to use as fuel. It is a serious and life-threatening condition. The hospital staff began to give Jason insulin, but had a very hard time finding a vein that would take the IV. His body was starting to shut down. He couldn't answer any questions the doctor asked, like what was his date of birth, who I was, or anything that he would normally easily answer.

Once they placed the IV in, and insulin started pumping into his system, Jason started doing a little better physically, but was still completely out of it mentally. The doctor updated me on his status. His blood sugar level was 850; the normal range should be less than 140 after eating. The doctor was surprised he was still alive and said the next 24-48 hours were critical.

My heart sank. The love of my life was deathly sick, and there was nothing I could do but pray. I felt helpless. Even though we had many visitors come to see him and check on him, I still felt so alone. I couldn't even imagine losing my husband and my best friend. Close family and friends prayed for Jason, and over the course of a week he finally improved enough to be out of ICU.

The doctors informed us that he would now be insulin-dependent, to watch out for any sign of DKA, and to take extra precautions if he became sick again. I was so thankful that he was going to be alright. I knew that God hadn't called him this far for him to die. Jason had a purpose and a calling to fulfill.

They released him from the hospital the same day the church would be voting on if he was to be the new pastor. Our prayer had been, "God, if this is your will for us, let the church vote for Jason to be the pastor. If it is not Your will, then let them vote against it."

The calling God had placed on our lives came to pass, and the church did vote Jason in as pastor of The Lighthouse UPC. We were so excited, and thankful for the huge responsibility, and trust that the church had in us to lead them. We thank God so much for all He has done, and especially for preserving my husband's life so that he may fulfill what God has in store for us.

## *Reflection*

Life has not always been easy, and there have been many times I have wanted to give up, but I thank God I never did. We have persevered through a lot of hard times and storms, but it has always been worth it.

Over the years, I have learned about people. There are people that are completely toxic to your spiritual life and want nothing but to see you fail. As hard as it has been, I have had to cut those people out of my life. Some have been family, and some have been people I thought of as friends. Not everyone is a friend and not everyone wants to see others succeed and prosper.

It hurts so much sometimes to know that the people you thought loved and cared for you are just waiting to see you fall so they can say, "I told you so."

I had to make a choice that there is no place for negativity in my life. I've had enough negativity in my past. God has brought me and my family too far and I have seen Him do too many great things to stop following Him now, or to let anyone hinder me from obeying Him.

I've learned we can each do anything in the world that we want to do. We can be anything that we want to be. I desire to be the best I can be for the little bit of time I have on earth. I want to be whatever God would like me to be. I hope I can at least change a few lives while I'm here and show people that God truly loves them more than anyone else ever will.

God never meant for anyone to go through a life of hurt and pain. John 10:10 says, He came so that we might have life, and have it more abundantly. Throughout my life, I have had some regrets about choices I've made, but living for God has never been one of them. No matter how many times I fall or fail Him, He still loves me and forgives me every time. He has blessed my life immensely with Jason, our amazing kids, friends, family, and our awesome church family. He has transformed my life for the better, the very least I can do is love and serve Him for the rest of my life.

CHAPTER 14

# *Broken & Beautiful*

JEREMIAH 18:4 KJV
And the vessel that he made of clay
was marred in the hand of the potter:
so he made it again another vessel,
as seemed good to the potter to make it.

My life is far from perfect. I go through trials and problems just like everyone else. The difference is, I am happy and content with my life. I am no longer in danger as I was in my past, living in fear every day.

I have a husband who loves and adores me. He can also still make me laugh until I cry. Have we ever struggled in our marriage? Yes, at times we have struggled, but we worked whatever problem we faced out together, and we came out stronger for it in the end. Jason is still my favorite preacher and my best friend.

Our children are growing up before our eyes. Our oldest three boys have graduated high school. We are so proud of the young men they have become and are praying that they let God have His way in them. They were brought up in truth and dedicated to God a long time ago. I have no doubt that they will fulfill whatever God has called for them to do in this lifetime.

Train up a child in the way he should go:
and when he is old, he will not depart from it.
PROVERBS 22:6

Our oldest son is now 21-years-old and a dad to our beautiful granddaughter, Eden Rose. She has absolutely turned our world upside down. We all adore her so very much. We have a wonderful relationship with her mom, who is like a daughter to us. I am now a "MiMi" and am loving every minute of it!

We raised our children to know that we would always love them. We all fall sometimes—we are only human—but God's grace and mercy is everlasting. He will always welcome each of us with open arms. As parents, we love our kids the same way. We will always be there for them. I have told them over and over again, "There is nothing that you can do, or any choice that you can make that will ever make me stop loving you. And that's how God loves us too."

All children need to know that they have endless love and emotional and spiritual support from their families. If they stray away from God's truth, that love may be the only thing that they hold onto that can bring them back home.

People often like to hang our faults and failures over our heads. That is the enemy's tactic to keep us from fulfilling what God has called us to do. Don't let what people say deter you from advancing to your fullest potential and using all your God-given talent to be an inspiration to others and to win the lost.

I'm so glad Jason came along and told me all about God. He befriended me and encouraged me. He let me know that I could be and do so much more than I had ever known. I hope that you can be that kind of encourager to someone else. You never know what God will do in their life through you.

I watched God transform my dad from a raging alcoholic into a loving father and grandfather. God instantly delivered my dad from crack, and he later received the Holy Ghost with the evidence of speaking in other tongues.

I have a wonderful relationship with my mom and my dad, and I know they will always be there for me. They have always supported me in my walk with God, and for that I will forever be grateful.

I have seen God transform my sister, Teresa, from a "party girl" into an amazing mother and the "favorite aunt" to all of our kids. She is one of my biggest supporters and one of my closest friends. I've seen my sister, Renee, overcome many things in her life that would have been impossible to overcome without God. Through her trials, I've seen her grow in strength and love toward God like never before. God desires to change and remakes each of us to be something greater than we were before; we only need to allow Him to do it.

Kintsugi is an old Japanese art form dating back for centuries. It requires a cracked and broken piece of pottery, so that it can be repaired with a special lacquer dusted with powered gold, silver, or platinum. The name "Kintsugi" literally translates to "golden joinery." The closely related word "*Kintsukuroi,*" means "golden repair." Where cracks once destroyed a ceramic piece, beautiful seams of gold glint now give a unique appearance to the piece.

An article I found online stated that "the repair method celebrates each artifact's unique history by emphasizing its fractures and breaks, instead of hiding or disguising them."

Kintsugi often makes the repaired piece even more beautiful than the original, revitalizing it with new life.

Just like Kintsugi pottery, Jesus takes all our broken pieces and places them back together so that the finished product is so much more beautiful than the original ever was.

He has remade me.

# About the Author
## Shannon Marie Dorsey

Shannon lives in Central Texas with her husband, Jason Dorsey, and their children, Edward James Salinas II, Noah Alexander Salinas, Joseph Anthony Salinas, Nathanael Tyrel Dorsey, and Miracle Marie Dorsey.

Jason and Shannon Dorsey have served in pastoral ministry at The Lighthouse UPC in Killeen, Texas since January of 2016.

She is an executive administrative assistant at a counseling and consulting company, and has an Associates Degree with focus in Psychology from Central Texas College.

For speaking engagements, contact her at 254.371.4350, or by email at ShannonMDorsey123@gmail.com.

"In writing this book, I hope to reach others that have gone through or are going through the difficulties of domestic violence. There is a life after abuse, and though at times it seems hopeless, there is always a way out.

"There is a loving and caring God that hears your prayers and cries for help. You can have a better life and you're worth is far above rubies, diamonds, or gold.

"I hope that in opening up and sharing my testimony, others will see that there is so much more waiting for them. You deserve better and deserve to be truly loved."

Jason and Shannon Dorsey

From left to right: Joseph, Nathanael, Noah, Jason and Shannon, Miracle, and Edward II.

CPSIA information can be obtained
at www.ICGtesting.com
Printed in the USA
LVHW040134250322
714345LV00006B/103